G

Gemini
1993

Teri King's complete horoscope
for all those whose birthdays fall between
22 May and 21 June

Ann happy
Reading
lots love
W

Pan Astral
London, Sydney and Auckland

Pan Astral regrets that it cannot enter
into any correspondence with readers requesting
information about their horoscope

First published 1992 by Pan Books Ltd,
Cavaye Place, London SW10 9PG

© Teri King 1992

ISBN 0 330 31795 4

9 8 7 6 5 4 3 2 1

Phototypeset by Intype, London
Printed in England by Clays Ltd, St Ives plc

This book is sold subject to the condition that it
shall not, by way of trade or otherwise, be lent, re-sold,
hired out, or otherwise circulated without the publisher's prior
consent in any form of binding or cover other than that in which
it is published and without a similar condition including this
condition being imposed on the subsequent purchaser

Contents

Introduction

Astrology is a very complex science. While it can be useful in assessing the different aspects of human relationships, there are many misconceptions associated with it. Not the least of these is the cynic's question: 'How can zodiac forecasts be accurate for all the millions of people born under any one sign?' The answer is that all horoscopes published in newspapers, books and magazines are, of necessity, of a general nature. Unless an astrologer can work from the date, time and place of your birth, the reading given will only be true for the typical member of your sign.

Take a person born on 1 May. This person is principally a subject of Taurus, simply because the Sun occupies that portion of the heavens known as Taurus during the period 21 April to 21 May. However, there are other influences to be taken into account, for instance the Moon: this planet enters a fresh sign every forty-eight hours. On the birth date in question it may have been in, say, Virgo – and if that were the case it would make this particular subject a Taurean/Virgoan. Then again the rising sign or Ascendant must also be taken into consideration. This also changes constantly, as approximately every two hours a new sign passes over the horizon. The rising sign is of utmost importance, determining the image projected by the subject to the outside world – in effect, the personality. (This is why the time of birth is essential for compiling a natal chart.) Let us suppose that in this particular instance Taurus was rising at the time of birth; this would make the individual a Taurean/Virgoan/Taurean. Now, because two of the three main influences are Taurus, the subject would be a fairly typical Taurean, displaying the faults and attributes associated with this sign. But if the Moon and the Ascendant were, say, in Aquarius, the subject would exhibit more of the vices and virtues of a true Aquarian.

For each of the nine planets this procedure is carried on, each making up a significant part of the subject's character; their positions, the signs they occupy, and the aspects formed from one to another all play a part of the make up. The calculation and interpretation of these movements, the work of the astrologer, will produce an individual's birth chart. Because the heavens are constantly changing, people with identical birth charts are a very rare occurrence, although it could happen with people born at the same time and in the same place. In such a case the deciding factors as to how those individuals differ in their lives, loves, careers, financial prospects and so on would be due to environmental and parental influences.

Returning to the hypothetical Taurean: as has been said he would believe himself typical of the sign; but were the Moon and the Ascendant in the alternative positions stated he would be an Aquarian. So he would get a more dependable reading from the general Aquarian predictions than from the Taurean ones. This explains why some people swear by their newspaper horoscopes, while others can never believe them. But whatever his Moon sign and Ascendant, the Taurean will always display certain characteristics of his birth sign, because of the Sun's influence.

Belief in astrology does not necessarily mean believing we lead totally determined lives, that we are 'fated', or that we have no control over our destiny. What it shows is that our lives run in cycles, for good and for bad; knowing this, with the help of astrology we can make the most of, or minimize, certain patterns and tendencies. How this is done is entirely up to the individual.

For instance, if you know beforehand that you have a lucky period ahead, you can make the most of it by pushing ahead with plans and aspirations – anything that is dear to you. It follows that you can also take more care in times of illness, misfortune, romantic upset and everyday adversity.

Astrology should be used as it was originally intended – as a guide, especially to character. Throughout the ages there has never been found a better guide to character analysis, enabling people to learn and use advantageously the information relating to personality, friendships, work and romance.

Once this invaluable information has been understood it makes it easier for us to see ourselves as we really are and, what's more, as others see us. We can accept our own weaknesses and limitations and those of others. We can evolve from there to inner peace and outer confidence.

In the following pages you will find character, happiness and partnership guides; romantic, health and marriage prospects; punters' luck; monthly and daily forecasts; and an indication of the Moon's influence on your moods. Used wisely, astrology can help you through life. It is not intended to encourage complacency, since in the final analysis it is all up to you. Allow astrology to walk hand in hand with you and success and happiness are virtually guaranteed.

Teri King

A New Look At Your Sun Sign

Most members of the general public appreciate that of necessity Sun sign astrology is fairly general, and that should an individual wish for a more in-depth study then it is essential to hire an astrologer who will proceed to study his client's date, year, place and time of birth. The birth chart is then correlated from the facts.

However, there is a middle way which can be most illuminating. Each Sun sign comprises 30° (or days), and by reducing these down into three sections it is possible to acquire a clearer picture of your sign which is more intimate than the usual method. Therefore, check out your date of birth and draw your own conclusions:

Gemini (22 May to 21 June)

If you were born between 22 May and 31 May, then your Sun falls in the Mercury section of Gemini. Your life is a battleground between your mind and your feelings, and too often your thoughts enslave you with a merciless force. Highly intelligent, you possess verbal talents which could lead to success in writing, teaching and all forms of communication. Because of your quick wits, you have the personality of the proverbial 'life and soul of the party' or the TV commentator who fully commands an audience. You are nervous, restless, talkative and gregarious; you enjoy a good laugh, and have the kind of sparkling sense of humour that is extremely attractive. Though friendly, you are very fickle when it comes to your feelings. You are cautious and critical where romance is concerned, and rarely fall in love but creep into your commitments sideways, wondering all the time if you are doing the right thing. You analyse situations to the point where you start to wish someone could help you to switch off your mind and get on to something else. Insomnia is a lifelong problem, which has a tendency to torment you in the small hours. Anxiety, nervousness and worry are also pitfalls for a mind that works overtime. Physical activity is a must for a mind such as yours, and is probably something that you have always avoided like the plague. Deep down you believe that everything that isn't mental is really a waste of time. Once you learn how to liberate yourself from your mind, and to control it rather than letting it control you, you will see how limitless life is and how simply joy can be achieved.

For those with birth dates between 1 June and 11 June your Sun falls in part of Gemini ruled by Venus. You are charming, flirtatious, slyly romantic and extremely creative. Your verbal abilities can bring you recognition in the area of fiction as well as in creative journalism. Since you are never at a loss for words, you make a highly successful public speaker and have the invincible charm of a comedienne who is at ease performing. You have great enthusiasm, which you can successfully utilize in both public relations and show business. A logical mind combined with your charisma could give you the ability to be anything from an entertainer to a literary agent, to a television writer. You are an elegant host or hostess and – since you tend to be something of a snob – your parties are always populated by 'the right people'. No one can deny that you are a delight to have around. You have a stellar sense of humour and a *joie de vivre* that imbues you with much more personal power than you may give yourself credit for. Allow your artistic sensitivity to have disciplined expression and you may find that success is not far away.

If you were born between 12 June and 21 June, your Sun sign is in the part of Gemini inhabited by Uranus. Of all the Geminis, you are the most freedom-loving and unconventional. You prefer many ongoing relationships to a monogamous situation, and have a restless erratic nature – but often a brilliant and original mind. You are attracted to the areas of film and television, as well as computers. However, you also have the aptitude to become anything from an astrologer to a psychotherapist to an inventor. You are changeable, love anything new, lose interest in people fast and have an experimental attitude towards sex. It is difficult for you to be faithful to one person until later in life – and even then you may experience many temptations. In any marriage or love relationship, you need plenty of room, as claustrophobia sets in quickly. You are a 'people person', and a partygoer. Open-minded and witty, on occasions you are a trifle unstable in the way you lead your life. You are well-meaning, but often undependable until well into middle age. Of all Geminis you are the most highly-strung, nervous and anxiety-ridden. You need to be very disciplined about how you use your energies or they may diffuse into many half-finished projects,

11

conversations and good intentions that never seem to get very far.

What Makes Geminians Happy?

In order to achieve a happy state, Geminians need the constant mental activity of stimulating company. Being madly in love helps and they lap it up when sexual advances are made at parties. They are delighted when they discover a new interest, or when they are doing almost nothing in the sunshine (a Geminian never does *absolutely* nothing). Being happy also means getting a good night's sleep at last, learning from someone who is considered much brighter or finding that one of their myriad ideas successfully takes off. They love it when remarks are made about their youthful faces or figures and as parents they rejoice when a child does better at school than expected. They are further delighted when confronted with any kind of change or when they have solved a problem – from a crossword to something in real life. Playing with their children's toys at Christmas brings great pleasure, but mostly Geminians are happiest when there are not enough hours in the day.

What Makes Geminians Unhappy?

They are miserable when they can't sleep, something which is always elusive; when their intelligence is questioned; when they are bored or ill. Unhappiness comes from being lumbered at a party with the 'bore of the year'; when friends demand more attention than *they* are receiving; and when duty visits to relatives are expected. Routine in any guise makes them unhappy too – also if friends fail to turn off the television when they call. They are positively wretched if they forget to change their library books and then find they have read everything in the house including the labels on the bottles. Other things Geminians loathe include being humiliated in public or finding that a loved one has betrayed a confidence. They may be flighty and flirtatious, but as the song says, they are 'always true to you, darling, in my fashion'.

Partnerships

Gemini Woman

With Aries Man (21 March to 20 April)

This man's strength of character, independence and outer confidence could impress her. She may like his quick decisive manner and love of business, coupled with his constant search for new ideas, and feel it compatible with her own rather erratic personality. Later, however, it will become apparent that their lack of shared interests gives rise to conflict and irritation. She will not like the way he assumes the role of leader; she likes to do things her way. Also, she has no time for his interest in sports and, similarly, he shows no liking for her artistic pursuits. However, as both have short memories, anger and argument will soon be forgotten, though he will remain vindictive a while longer than she. He will never be able to understand this complex creature and the partnership will soon dissolve into a cool separation.

With Taurus Man   (21 April to 21 May)

Romantic fancy is what could initially draw these two very different characters together, for whilst she is in this frame of mind he will seem quite attractive to her. However, he is noted for being a rather slow, conservative character and this characteristic will eventually grate on her nerves, for she is all speed and quickness of thought and action. She likes change and experimentation, he doesn't, and this she will see as stubborn short-sightedness. She also feels that life has a bit more to offer than a steady home life; he will soon find this out and this could be the breaking point. Their shared artistic loves will not be enough to hold this relationship together.

With Gemini Man   (22 May to 21 June)

If there is a lack of strength on either side of this relationship it is doomed to disaster; otherwise it could be an excellent union. He will understand that she has a deep need for partnership on a high plane and, in matters of the intellect, they are in accord.

This man is one of the very few who can be friend, lover and companion all wrapped into one. However, he will grow to rely on her maternal instinct to satisfy his childlike tendencies. She too can be this way inclined, and therefore, like children, arguments could develop over the silliest of things. Their love will have to be very deep for them to sustain too much friction in everyday life.

With Cancer Man   (22 June to 22 July)
The home-loving Cancer will certainly be upset by this woman's love of a hectic social life. He likes to ignore the world in favour of his home life, and she could consider herself a virtual prisoner of this character's domesticity. It is highly unlikely that she will ever be able to adjust to his house-proud way of life. She could be attracted to his peaceful nature, his readiness to join in and encourage her sense of fun and the endless compliments, but all this is hardly likely to make for a stable relationship, for she is, basically, fairly insensitive where returning these things is concerned. This man's life is motivated by his emotions, hers by her intellect. Whilst this could be what is known as a 'meaningful relationship' it is not one recommended for marriage.

With Leo Man   (23 July to 23 August)
The Gemini woman is constantly probing and enquiring and, if she digs beneath the Leo's arrogance, pride and over-demanding exterior, she could find a warm-hearted, affectionate human being. He likes to be an influence on those around him and, whilst she is not too keen on being told what to do, she could, on occasions, allow him to influence her in some directions. He will show respect for her individual freedom, but will demand, in return, praise, flattery and admiration. They both like the limelight and she could resent his obtaining too much of it, overshadowing her vivacity. Whilst he cannot comprehend her speedy changes of mood, she will find no good reason for his phases of laziness. However, her neurotic outbursts will be forgiven by this expansive man. Therefore, to make this relationship work, and it so often does, adaptability is the keyword.

With Virgo Man   (24 August to 23 September)
Realizing that the Virgo man is the type who will do virtually anything for the woman he loves, who can also provide the necessary intellectual stimulation she craves and is also entirely dependable, the Gemini woman could be attracted. Later, however, his sensible and logical character will tend to irritate. Also, Virgo has a rather petty attitude towards financial affairs, almost to the point of penny-pinching, and this will not suit her at all. Both are critical characters and their eagle eyes will often

16

be turned on each other, magnifying faults. He might also find her too vain and chaotic. This relationship is likely to be short-lived because he will soon begin to doubt her ability to love for any length of time. This will severely affect his self-confidence.

With Libra Man   (24 September to 23 October)
This is, generally speaking, a very good union. Both Libra and Gemini are Air signs so there is a basic compatibility to start with. They will share similar attitudes to emotions and things of the mind. They both have a need for personal freedom and an active social life, and also have a shared love of change. However, it is quite likely that he will want to lead his own life rather more than she, and she will have to endeavour to make him feel independent. There could be friction where his laziness is concerned, but she will be impressed by his frequent bursts of energy. Her displays of childish temperament will lead to his thinking her rather unfeminine in this quarter, but not other-wise. This relationship should be rewarding as both partners recognize the need to work at any union.

With Scorpio Man   (24 October to 22 November)
Scorpio is well known for his penetrating, investigative nature. It will not be long before he not only uncovers the good things about Miss Gemini, but also the bad things. She may try the same tactic on him, but to no avail, he will remain a complete mystery to her. Self-expression is not one of his attributes. Scorpio is also known for his jealous character, and he will not take lightly to her flirting and obvious enjoyment of stimulating company. He needs to show his woman that he is her protector, and he will show this by action rather than words. This jealous streak will appal her and the resultant possessiveness will cramp her style almost to the point of feeling imprisoned. With two such different outlooks this relationship is certainly destined for the rocks.

With Sagittarius Man   (23 November to 21 December)
Miss Gemini will find it easy to fall in love with this freedom-loving individual; the thing she will find hard to do is to make it last. Although this man is full of fun and life, his need for personal freedom differs from hers. He has to be able to live his life exactly as he wishes, free to do what he pleases. She, on the other hand, only needs to do that which is forbidden to her, or restricted in any way. He will be strongly attracted to

her, however, for he needs her ability to converse, learn and observe as this complements his own personality. He will still give her much attention even after they have been together for a long period, but he will insist on the truth at all times, and some of his truths could very well hurt her. He will tell her when he has been with another woman, for instance. This union will be highly complex.

With Capricorn Man   (22 December to 20 January)
Two characters further apart would be hard to find. He is a reserved, practical, sometimes over-serious individual, she a butterfly-brained, highly-strung, fun-loving character. He needs a woman who will take an interest and encourage him in his work, for this is a very important part of his life. Being a natural chatterbox, it will be difficult for her to be able to listen to this man when he has problems to discuss, but only in this way can she hope to relieve his tensions that lead to deep depression. He will be able to curb her restlessness, and will be quite content to let her make her own career as long as it does not interfere with his own. The aesthetic side of life will be shared and enjoyed. He is financially minded, thinking only of the future – Miss Gemini only thinks of her present needs, seeing no point in looking further ahead. This could be a major stumbling block in a very difficult relationship.

With Aquarius Man   (21 January to 19 February)
This is a relationship that will have at its base the need for intellectual rapport. The physical side of love will hardly enter into things. They will probably agree on the necessity for a constantly changing circle of friends and interests. However, his continual need to help others in distress, whilst ignoring her needs, could lead to irritation and not a little friction. His outside interests will always interfere with the domestic side of life. This situation will lead to much argument, for he will not be able to understand her anxiety over what he sees as a trivial matter. He will always be totally honest with her as their relationship deepens and he will show an interest in everything she does. This is a good union although it is based mainly on intellectual compatibility.

With Pisces Man   (20 February to 20 March)
Two double-sided characters leads to four personalities involved in this relationship. He can be bursting with logical, positive

thinking one day and withdrawn, secretive and illogical the next. One side of her character will fall in love with one side of his character. This will be fine whilst both compatible characters are showing, but when they are not, then the trouble begins. She will have to respect his need to escape into his own secret world in order to plan or to solve his problems; she will also have to refrain from applying pressure for this kind of man backs away from such behaviour. If life should deal him a cruel blow, she will need to be there in order to comfort and offer security. If she fails him he will drift into the wide blue yonder. This makes for a very shaky union.

Gemini Man

With Aries Woman (21 March to 20 April)

By virtue of his irrepressible nature, Mr Gemini could be something of a mystery to Miss Aries. She will be totally thrown by his tendency to be exalted one moment and in the depths of despair the next. This good-looking, sociable type may initially attract her, but in the end she could lose him through her desire to be the dominant partner. This he will rebel against, not waiting around for the result of such a battle. He may return later, but only if he is certain that he will not be pushed around again. The Gemini man needs to be constantly stimulated mentally and, although she may not want to look after him and get him to be more sensible, she will not be able to provide the stimulation needed. This affair could end quite suddenly when she finds that she has a totally bored individual on her hands. She will need to develop her imagination if she is to hang on to the Gemini.

With Taurus Woman (21 April to 21 May)

The Gemini man is full of charm and a pleasant childishness that could appeal, initially, to Miss Taurus. However, before becoming deeply involved with this character she would be wise to let things hang fire for a while. It would be only too easy for her to allow a wild infatuation to be mistaken for the real thing. She should try to keep her artistic interests to herself, unless of course she is up to professional standard – then he may be impressed. She had also better keep hidden her talents as a homemaker, the very last thing Mr Gemini wants to feel is domesticated. He must have his freedom in order to function

19

correctly. However, she is bound not to understand his need to flirt on social occasions, and the resulting jealousy could put the tin hat on this relationship.

With Gemini Woman   (22 May to 21 June)

If there is a lack of strength on either side of this relationship it is doomed to disaster, otherwise it could be an excellent union. He will understand that she has a deep need for partnership on a high plane and, in matters of the intellect, they are in accord. This man is one of the very few who can be friend, lover and companion all wrapped into one; however, he will grow to rely on her maternal instinct to satisfy his childlike tendencies. She, too, can be this way inclined, and therefore, like children, arguments can develop over the silliest of things. Their love will have to be very deep for them to sustain too much friction in everyday life.

With Cancer Woman   (22 June to 22 July)

His zest for living, his charm and a gift for communication will initially appeal to Cancer. She will, however, know at the back of her mind that they are quite different basically. The Gemini is unable to pursue a train of thought for any length of time; constant stimulation and a need for novelty are his driving forces. She likes a quiet homely and domestic situation and his ways are bound to intrude into this ideal. She also likes to cling to her objects of love, and this will not suit the freedom-loving Gemini; he doesn't like to be possessed. His moods, whilst being superficial are also changeable, but hers go much deeper and it is difficult to lift her out of them. The Gemini man is capable of outrageous flirting and, whilst meaning no real harm, this will destroy the loving, sensitive Cancer. This is a very difficult relationship due to the opposing personalities involved.

With Leo Woman   (23 July to 23 August)

These two characters could get very involved in a short space of time. He will introduce her to, and involve her in, a hectic social whirl. However, Leo does have the need to dominate this relationship and very soon this will begin to make itself apparent. He may not take this too seriously at first, but there will come a time when he will rebel at her efforts to run his life. This woman will not understand his need for mental stimulation, nor his deep need to communicate and find out about other people. She will, on occasion, display a fiery love and passion that will give him security in their romance, but he will eventually come to feel smothered by this intense emotion. The more he pulls away the more she will try to hang on until the relationship bursts apart at the seams. Pressure through trying to live together will be the eventual destroyer of this union.

With Virgo Woman   (24 August to 23 September)
This man's childlike appeal could attract the more mature Virgo woman. His versatility, his need to communicate could well appeal to the mercurial mind of Miss Virgo. She too needs mental stimulation. However, she will later come to the conclusion that a restless soul is her lot, and she will try to change him. He must never be aware of the fact that she is trying to introduce a steadying element into his life; this he will regard as interference with his freedom and will try to escape as quickly as possible. She has a love of routine and he a preference for chaos, so clashes here will be unavoidable. Her well-run day to day existence will eventually make him feel restricted and he will opt out. Not a good relationship.

With Libra Woman   (24 September to 23 October)
The main factor that brings these two characters together will be the love of novelty and excitement. Initially they will be forever rushing about enjoying themselves and indulging in activity of all kinds. Somewhere along the line she will begin to wonder about his irresponsible behaviour. Finances, too, will giver her cause for concern as it will be left up to her to introduce some stability. If he should notice an air of practicality entering her life, she will begin to lose some of her appeal, so this should always be done surreptitiously. Eventually she will come to resent the fact that it is she who always has to accommodate his moods and ideas, never the other way around. He will, however, offer encouragement and enthusiasm should she be involved in her own career. If he can cultivate the ability to listen to others, their relationship will benefit. They are both attracted to travel and many spur-of-the-moment trips will be enjoyed. This could be an excellent partnership.

With Scorpio Woman   (24 October to 22 November)
A combination of characters that is best avoided. Once she has started a relationship with this character she will be reluctant to let go and allow him any personal freedom, she will want to take complete possession. Should he air his opposing views to

this state of affairs there will be a scene that can only be described as emotional. Her need for financial security will be threatened by this man, as will her need for a calm existence. The irresponsible side to his character, his restlessness, can be relied upon to create a deep rift in the relationship. Given sufficient time, he will come to regard her as neurotic, bigoted and a millstone around his neck.

With Sagittarius Woman (23 November to 21 December)
The emphasis in this relationship has to be on fun and novelty. These are two of the most intelligent and communicative, sun-loving signs of the zodiac and both their minds need constant exercise. Both attract friends and there will be little time spent alone in their own home. They enjoy uncomplicated, free lives and this will keep them contented and happy for a while. However, finances will need someone to look after them, but the problem will be, who? Neither will wish to take the reins in this area. It would also be difficult to imagine either of them in one job for very long as they both like constant change. This could be a good relationship for a short period, but it would be unwise for any length of time.

With Capricorn Woman (22 December to 20 January)
Attitudes to life are so contrary that it is difficult to imagine these two being together for more than a few weeks. She would prefer to look life directly in the eye and face it practically; the Gemini likes to play-act and live life on impulse. He is unable to face up to reality, even if he has to do so, and no amount of nagging on her part will alter this situation. She could become motherly towards such an immature man, building up his ego when he is down and soothing his wounds when the world has treated him badly. She is subject to depression, and this he will share for a while. Then he will expect her to snap out of it as quickly as he can change his moods. This is impossible for her; she needs to climb out from under the black cloud slowly. She must expect to take the lead in financial matters for he is incapable of saving or worrying about the next penny.

With Aquarius Woman (21 January to 19 February)
There is a love of communication in this relationship and it will not be long before they are totally involved with each other. They could become totally absorbed in each other's interests and a lot of fun will be had. Gemini is the original jack of all

trades and this will make finding a job rather difficult; the Aquarian also has tendencies in this direction which can, of course, lead to financial problems. A switching of roles could take place, each alternately becoming the bread-winner. She will have to decide, in the end, how the finances are to be handled and, providing she accepts this role, then the relationship could be very happy and stimulating for both parties.

With Pisces Woman   (20 February to 20 March)

The possession of grasshopper minds makes these two attractive to each other, but when she realizes that he needs to exercise his mental abilities on the opposite sex she will be consumed with jealousy; much friction will arise from this direction. Her possessiveness is another thing he will rebel against for he doesn't consider this to be a part of love. Both characters have changeable moods and this could further make the relationship exhausting and complex. Both will want to have their own separate careers and as there will be no one to look after financial matters, this will eventually be the breaking point. Debt collectors could be frequent visitors to their household. This relationship, though shaky, could succeed, though it will be fairly nerve-racking. The ability to endure turmoil is not strong in either character and a long relationship needs careful consideration.

Astrological Guide to Eating Habits

Once the festive period is well and truly behind us, many will find they have been lumbered with a few extra pounds – and in some unlucky instances . . . stones! How can astrology help? Well, though obesity may in some instances have a physical basis, it is now widely believed that when we reach for that extra cream-bun or cake, we are in fact compensating for something lacking in our lives. Astrologically, there are weaknesses in all of us which when stimulated will make us head for the fridge door.

Read about your astrological characteristics and see if you can beat your own particular devil.

Fortunately for Geminians, most members of this sign manage to retain their sylph-like figure even into advanced years; this is mainly due to that nervous energy which simply burns away the fat. There are of course exceptions, and the fat ones are a complete contradiction to the old adage that a fat person is a jolly person. The reason an overweight Gemini has found it necessary to indulge his or her appetite to excess is generally boredom. Those born under this sign have to keep active heads; that means constant stimulation, and when this is not forthcoming they are a miserable sight to behold. Therefore, when subjected to routine or uninteresting work – or even dreary mates – some Geminians will eat simply to keep themselves occupied. Far better then to develop a new interest or to pick up a book – either of which will keep those unwanted inches away.

Love Prospects 1993

Have you ever wondered why suddenly for no apparent reason you lose interest in love and in sex? No? Don't pretend that it never happens to you. Let me refresh that grey matter.

There you are after a couple of sexually, or romantically, hectic weeks considering applying for the lover-of-the-year award when, quite suddenly, the TV becomes more attractive than any member of the opposite sex you have seen for some time. Could it be connected with your birth sign? Yes, it most certainly can. Venus and Mars are the planets that count.

Favourably placed, they improve your looks, vitality and zest for living, but when they gang up on you, you have about as much confidence in yourself as King Kong at a beauty contest! Your nerves jangle and mentally, you are preoccupied with external matters. But not to worry, your sex appeal will return. It is simply a matter of time. The table opposite has been compiled in order to prepare you for your romantically active periods.

How to interpret the table

1 HEART – poor. If you try hard, someone of the opposite sex may decide to go out with you, but it is going to be hard work.
2 HEARTS – fair. If your lover has nothing better to do, then you may be lucky, but you will need to make the move.
3 HEARTS – good. Watch out, you are getting some mighty strange looks. Whoops! Well I did warn you! It is a pretty hot time.
4 HEARTS – wow! Take cover, unless you want to be caught in the stampede.

Your Love Chart for 1993

	Jan	Feb	Mar	Apr	May	June	July	Aug	Sept	Oct	Nov	Dec
Aries	♥	♥♥♥♥	♥♥♥♥	♥♥♥♥	♥♥♥♥	♥♥♥	♥♥	♥♥	♥	♥♥♥	♥♥	♥♥♥
Taurus	♥♥	♥	♥♥	♥♥	♥	♥♥♥♥	♥♥♥	♥♥	♥♥	♥♥	♥♥♥	♥
Gemini	♥	♥	♥♥	♥	♥♥	♥	♥♥♥	♥♥♥	♥♥♥	♥	♥	♥♥♥♥
Cancer	♥♥♥♥	♥	♥	♥	♥	♥♥	♥	♥♥	♥	♥♥♥	♥♥♥	♥
Leo	♥	♥♥	♥	♥♥	♥	♥	♥♥	♥	♥♥♥♥	♥	♥	♥♥♥
Virgo	♥♥♥♥	♥♥♥♥	♥	♥♥♥	♥	♥♥♥♥	♥	♥♥	♥♥♥♥	♥♥♥♥	♥♥♥	♥
Libra	♥	♥	♥♥	♥♥	♥♥♥♥	♥	♥♥♥	♥	♥♥♥	♥♥♥	♥	♥♥
Scorpio	♥♥♥	♥	♥♥	♥♥	♥	♥♥♥♥	♥♥♥♥	♥	♥♥	♥	♥♥♥♥	♥
Sagittarius	♥	♥	♥	♥	♥♥	♥♥	♥♥♥	♥♥	♥♥	♥♥	♥	♥♥♥♥
Capricorn	♥♥	♥♥	♥♥	♥♥	♥	♥♥	♥	♥♥♥	♥♥♥	♥	♥♥	♥♥♥
Aquarius	♥	♥	♥	♥	♥♥	♥♥	♥♥	♥	♥♥	♥♥♥	♥	♥♥
Pisces	♥	♥	♥♥	♥	♥♥	♥	♥♥	♥♥♥	♥♥♥♥	♥	♥♥♥	♥

Health Year 1993

We all have our accident-prone days. You know the kind of thing: you get out of bed and walk into the bedroom door, fall down the stairs, trip over the cat, burn your hands on the kettle and then, finally, as you rush out of the door to catch that important train you discover that it is Sunday! Does this sound familiar? Of course. There are also other days when, for no apparent reason, you wake up with nerves jangling. The slightest noise, like the rustle of a newspaper, and you are reaching for the tranquillizers! Could this have anything to do with astrology? Yes.

Each physical ailment is a symptom of a bad aspect from Mars, Venus, Jupiter, et cetera. The table opposite has been compiled in order for you to check out your bad weeks, and with any luck prepare for them.

How to interpret the table

THE HAMMER – This is the symbol of the headache. Possibly caused by tension, toothache or simply a hangover.

THE WARNING – Watch out – those nerves will be easily shredded. Put in your ear plugs and hope for the best.

BLACK CLOUD – Depression. There will be a tendency for you during this week to feel that the end of the world is nigh. Take constructive steps to keep yourself occupied.

BANDAGED FINGER – Accident prone. Anything from a cut finger to a sore heel.

THE APPLE – Relax – you are hale and hearty.

Your Health Chart 1993

Money Year 1993

Astrologically speaking, certain years are luckier for some signs than others. Some people simply seem to have been born lucky, while others struggle for most of their lives and achieve very little. Moreover, your luck can come in patches. For example, you are just beginning to pull yourself out from down under when bang! an unexpected or overlooked bill lands on your doormat. Alternatively, you lay down your 'masterplan' for the future, hardly daring to hope it will work, then to your delight along comes promotion or a raise and your bank manager smiles on you – for once.

When it comes to cash, there are many variations on the theme, and how good any one year is likely to be depends on the state of your money planet. This chart has been compiled so that during the more difficult times you will be able to see the light at the end of the proverbial tunnel, while also being alert to lucky periods and able to take advantage of them. Remember that for some, good and bad fortune comes in never-ending phases, while for others precarious living seems the norm.

How to interpret the table

THE LADDER – In general this indicates a lucky phase. You will certainly be holding your own during this time and there may even be chances to better your position – perhaps promotion or a raise.

QUESTION MARK – Time to re-think your strategy. You can do this by discussing your affairs with the bank manager, your accountant or perhaps the family. A spare-time job or new budget may be the answer.

LIGHTNING – A period when you are inspired and Lady Luck strikes out of the blue. Sudden gains are possible through speculation, an unexpected opportunity or maybe a competition win. Any ideas you have for bettering your life are worth considering.

THE BILL – Don't take this too literally. While you may be in debt at this stage, the symbol also warns that you may be in danger of exercising bad judgement or over-extending yourself, and that things may not be too rosy in the near future unless you are careful.

Your Money Chart 1993

	1st week	2nd week	3rd week	4th week
Jan	?	BILL	⚡	🪜
Feb	BILL	?	🪜	🪜
Mar	BILL	?	⚡	⚡
Apr	?	BILL	🪜	🪜
May	🪜	⚡	BILL	?
June	BILL	?	🪜	🪜
July	BILL	⚡	⚡	🪜
Aug	?	BILL	⚡	🪜
Sept	🪜	🪜	🪜	⚡
Oct	⚡	🪜	BILL	🪜
Nov	?	BILL	⚡	⚡
Dec	?	🪜	🪜	?

Uranus and Your Sex Appeal

Are you magnetically attractive to the opposite sex and other people? Have you a compelling determination and indomitable inner will? Do you like to take part in revolutionary causes? Have you a kind of genius for whatever it is you do? Are you interested in new inventions or original ideas? For the clues to this behaviour you should consult the planet Uranus. It is important for everyone who wants to foresee events and dominate their environment to understand the position of Uranus in their own particular horoscope.

Uranus in Aries

You have Uranus in Aries if you were born between the following dates:

31 March 1927 to 4 November 1927
13 January 1928 to 6 June 1934
10 October 1934 to 27 March 1935

Uranus in Aries gives the will to dominate and lead; there is great fire and independence of spirit. These individuals have an inner urge for supremacy, and they brook no opposition; when thwarted their tempers can be explosive. They consider it a positive affront when others differ with them and deal with such persons accordingly.

For such people, their will and their head are as one. They often have a fixed idea that is compatible with their inner drive, and if Uranus is in a strong position in their horoscope, they will concentrate all their forces on realizing their ambitions and convincing the world about their ideas. Nevertheless, while equally strong their will is not as consistent as Uranus in Capricorn and Taurus, since they become bored with a particular project for no apparent reason and then turn all their energy towards realizing some entirely different goal. This in turn may occupy them for some time, but they are likely to drop it just as suddenly.

Therefore, while possessing a certain enterprising spirit and true courage, it is hard for such people to build consistently. This characteristic gives them the ability to attract easily, but not to maintain interest in the opposite sex.

Famous people with this position:

Edward Kennedy	Anne Bancroft
Leslie Caron	Fidel Castro
Audrey Hepburn	Jaqueline Kennedy

Uranus in Taurus

You have Uranus in Taurus if you were born between the following dates:

6 June 1934 to 9 October 1934
27 March 1935 to 7 August 1941
5 October 1941 to 14 May 1942

Uranus in Taurus is a position *par excellence* for remarkable will-power and determination, the inner drive being expressed in the most positive ways. The desire is to build, but whether this is to further some high ideal or to achieve a more material goal depends on the rest of the horoscope. In some cases, this position can impart a magnetic and distinctive quality to the singing voice, and can be an asset for those who take up the acting profession. When afflicted, it can result in some irritation of the throat. Uranus gives a prodigious amount of energy and the will to act is monumental; this may account for Guy de Maupassant's extensive works, George Bernard Shaw's plays, Napoleon's urge to build empires and Sigmund Freud's labours on psychoanalysis. Such men are typical of the giants this placing of Uranus can produce.

Amongst the less famous, the position bestows great firmness, diligence and patience. There is also present a dogged determination to be constructive, whatever the field.

If your Sun is in Taurus, Virgo or Capricorn, then people will be attracted to you like flies; to some extent this may irritate you, for you do not always enjoy being the centre of attraction.

Famous people with this position:

Julie Christie	Julie Andrews
Jane Fonda	Connie Francis
George Bernard Shaw	John Lennon
Warren Beatty	

Uranus in Gemini

You have Uranus in Gemini if you were born between the following dates:

8 August 1941 to 5 October 1941
14 May 1942 to 29 August 1948
12 November 1948 to 9 June 1949

It is through ideas rather than actions that you express your inner drive. Gentle and intellectual when it comes to persuading others to do your will, your strongest urges usually express themselves by means of the spoken and written word rather than through actual physical force. There are of course exceptions, such as Muhammad Ali, but even he exerted his will by the deft, rapid movements of his fists, which are ruled by Gemini. Gemini can also affect the voice and its magnetism in singers, actors or orators is evident. In art the expression can be linear and highly intellectual, as in the case of Toulouse-Lautrec.

If Uranus is badly aspected in your horoscope, you may be somewhat ineffectual in getting your own way, but when well-aspected you may express yourself successfully as a writer, teacher, journalist, lawyer, scientist, musician or in any occupation where cleverness with your mind, voice or fingers is important.

Famous people with this position:

Hayley Mills
Prince Charles
Brenda Lee
Mia Farrow

Geraldine Chaplin
Paul McCartney
George Harrison

Uranus in Cancer

You have Uranus in Cancer if you were born between the following dates:

30 August 1948 to 11 November 1948
20 June 1949 to 24 August 1955
28 January 1956 to 9 June 1956

Your deepest inner urges tend to be passive rather than active. You obey the dictates of your subconscious, and are sensitive and receptive rather than positive and strong-willed. In negative types this gives a very placid disposition; chameleon-like, these people assume the colours of their environment. Others can be highly developed on a psychic plane. With Uranus in Cancer will-power is not particularly aggressive, unless the Sun is in Taurus, Leo, Scorpio or Aquarius. Even when the Uranian traits of magnetism and will are fully developed, as in the case of Gandhi for example, leadership takes the form of passive resistance rather than openly declared war.

Among the less famous, there is a will to express themselves as gourmets, antique collectors or cooks. The men, as well as the women, have an urge to be homemakers and to mother the young, or they may desire to be mothered themselves and enjoy all the comforts of home. Many of you like to be popular, and you can be. In politics, literature or advertising you have the common touch, while in business you sense the public demand, especially when you deal in commodities for the home.

When Uranus is well-aspected, the artistic or musical sensibilities tend to be exquisite. When badly-aspected such people have explosive temperaments, disrupting their environments wilfully and arbitrarily. They are often a trial to their mothers in earlier years and subsequently disruptive in their own homes.

Famous people with this position:

Lord Byron   Henri Matisse
Bertrand Russell   Princess Anne

Uranus in Leo

You have Uranus in Leo if you were born between the following dates:

25 August 1955 to 27 January 1956
10 June 1956 to 1 November 1961
10 January 1962 to 9 August 1962

Uranus in this position, if afflicted, can bring trouble and obstacles to life, especially in youth: there will usually be some form of loss or privation, possibly through the father. These people display a disregard for convention, a great love of freedom and independence and a sometimes rebellious disposition, which can incur the dissatisfaction of superiors. Such individuals are fickle and changeable in love matters or, on the other hand, may suffer greatly from this trait in others.

Well-aspected, it is good for a public or professional career and much success may be achieved in this way. However, there may be social setbacks or annoyances, and hindrances through children. If your Sun is in Leo, Aries or Sagittarius then you have tremendous magnetism for others, but while you may bathe in the sunlight of popularity and carry a heavy engagement book you need to be far more cautious than other people when it comes to choosing a partner.

Famous people with this position:

John McEnroe   Jenny Agutter
Princess Caroline of Monaco   Tatum O'Neil

Uranus in Virgo

You have Uranus in Virgo if you were born between the following dates:

2 November 1961 to 9 January 1962
10 August 1962 to 23 June 1969

Uranus in Virgo makes you hyper-critical, and gives you unusual ideas about food and health which can lead to eccentric eating habits or 'quack cures', especially if this has been encouraged in early youth. However, it is an excellent placing for your intellectual ability and it is in fact through the mind that you attract other people. Lively, chatty and witty – ever ready with a clever retort – you are also subtle, penetrating, independent and original. You should succeed well in partnership or in association with other people.

Capricorns, Virgos and Taureans are strongly attracted to you physically. They may not necessarily be in the correct signs for marriage, but it is they who are drawn to you at the crook of your little finger.

Famous people with this position:

Tracy Austin   Lena Zavaroni
Brooke Shields

Uranus in Libra

You have Uranus in Libra if you were born between the following dates:

29 September 1968 to 21 May 1969
29 June 1969 to 20 November 1974
2 May 1975 to 7 September 1975

With Uranus in Libra you are split by the need to be true to your individuality while remaining loyal to the demands of society and others. Your personal freedom is at stake, so make your position known. Struggle valiantly to combine the best of both worlds in order to compromise.

It is likely that you will become aware of the differences separating you from the generation that preceded you. By then you will have devised a new formula that will re-establish the necessary sovereignty of the family unit and its value in providing order and guidance in the lives of those being born.

There is tremendous power and magnetism in your personality which can attract at an alarming rate. When you marry you will decide to limit the size of your family, not only to ensure that it receives the attention it deserves but also to allow you to enjoy a greater freedom to find personal fulfilment, probably through creative outlets.

Famous people with this position:

Bros

Uranus in Scorpio

You have Uranus in Scorpio if you were born between the following dates:

21 November 1974 to 1 May 1975
8 September 1975 to 16 February 1981
21 March 1981 to 15 November 1981

In this placing you are an extremely honest person, involved in the deeper subjects of existence such as death, sex and the spiritual continuity of life. Keen to learn all you can about everything, especially if it is considered taboo, you are unabashed and quite happy to ask questions because you do not fear the answers you may receive.

You are probably more aware of your spiritual commitment to others than those who profess to be but do not live up to their beliefs in terms of their actions. You have a personal, important destiny and it is on you that future generations will depend for the honesty that will allow the world to progress to new heights of awareness, enjoying a greater degree of development through personal and spiritual enlightenment.

On a more personal level you will quickly discover that other people are either fascinated – almost hypnotized – by you, or else totally repulsed. There will be no middle way, and this you must accept at an early age. To many, you are overwhelmingly irresistible. Make sure you do not misuse this wonderful gift.

Famous people with this position:

None to date.

Punters' Luck for 1993

Jockeys for the 1993 Flat Racing Season – Lucky Dates

Gambling is always a precarious business of course, and the following has been compiled in order to help the regular race-goer to minimize his or her losing bets.

The dates given are the good days shown on the jockey's birth chart.

WILLIE CARSON March 22nd (early afternoon), 27th; April 13th, 20th, 29th; May 2nd, 6th (late afternoon), 13th, 14th, 17th, 18th, 25th, 29th, 30th*; June 2nd, 7th, 14th, 17th, 22nd, 29th, 30th*; July 1st, 14th*, 15th, 17th, 27th; August 1st, 8th, 15th 16th, 17th (late afternoon), 22nd, 29th (early afternoon), 30th (evening); September 1st, 2nd, 6th (evening), 13th, 16th, 25th*, 29th (early afternoon); October 2nd, 5th, 9th, 11th, 13th, 17th; November 1st, 4th.

STEVE CAUTHEN March 23rd, 30th (late afternoon); April 2nd, 14th, 19th (late afternoon), 21st, 22nd, 23rd*; May 5th*, 9th, 24th, 30th; June 9th, 10th, 19th–21st inclusive, 26th*, 30th (late afternoon); July 4th*, 9th (late afternoon), 10th (early afternoon), 22nd, 25th, 29th*; August 4th (late afternoon), 9th–11th inclusive, 12th*, 13th, 26th*; September 5th (late afternoon), 10th, 13th, 20th–23rd inclusive, 24th*, 26th*; October 8th, 9th, 17th–20th inclusive, 31st; November 1st, 2nd.

RAY COCRANE March – nil; April 9th (early afternoon), 13th, 14th, 16th, 17th, 23rd*, 26th, 28th (late afternoon); May 2nd*, 7th*, 10th, 23rd (late afternoon); June 3rd*, 5th (early afternoon), 7th (evening), 20th, 22nd, 27th, 28th; July 1st, 3rd–7th inclusive, 12th, 19th (early afternoon), 20th*; August 1st*, 8th*, 10th, 25th*, 26th, 28th (evening); September 1st*, 2nd, 7th, 23rd, 26th, 29th; October 9th (evening), 10th*, 13th, 15th, 20th*, 24th, 29th (late afternoon); November 3rd, 5th, 6th, 7th*.

MICHAEL HILLS March 29th–31st inclusive; April 7th, 15th, 23rd, 24th, 28th; May 3rd, 4th, 10th*, 22nd, 24th, 27th (early afternoon); June 2nd, 3rd, 6th, 9th (late afternoon), 11th*, 12th,

18th, 26th; July 12th*, 16th, 18th*; August 1st*, 2nd, 13th*, 19th, 23rd (late afternoon), 31st*; September 3rd, 6th, 9th*, 12th, 13th, 19th; October 1st, 2nd, 11th, 13th*, 19th, 31st*; November 4th, 6th*.

RICHARD HILLS March 29th (late), 30th (early afternoon); April 3rd (late afternoon), 8th*, 11th*, 13th, 15th, 25th (early afternoon); May 11th, 14th, 20th, 27th*, 28th; June 1st, 7th*, 9th, 15th, 24th, 27th*, 29th; July 5th, 6th, 9th, 14th*, 28th; August 13th*, 17th, 21st, 27th, 30th; September 5th, 12th, 14th*; October 23rd, 26th; November 1st.

ERNIE JOHNSON March 29th; April 6th, 8th, 11th, 13th, 17th, 18th, 28th; May 6th (early afternoon), 10th, 12th–14th inclusive, 25th, 27th*, 29th; June 10th*, 13th, 16th, 21st (late afternoon), 27th; July 11th, 12th, 14th, 17th, 21st, 25th*, 29th, 30th, 31st*; August 12th*, 14th*, 16th, 17th, 18th*, 27th, 30th (early afternoon); September 4th, 5th, 12th*, 23rd*, 26th, 27th*; October 7th, 8th, 12th*, 14th, 18th, 21st, 31st*; November 1st, 2nd, 7th.

MICHAEL KINANE March 21st, 22nd; April 2nd, 3rd, 5th, 9th, 13th, 20th, 22nd; May 2nd, 3rd, 13th, 20th, 21st*, 23rd*, 25th; June 2nd, 3rd, 6th, 8th, 10th, 21st*, 24th, 26th; July 11th, 12th, 15th 17th; August 2nd, 4th, 5th, 7th, 8th, 12th*, 23rd, 25th*, 29th; September 5th, 11th, 12th*, 21st, 22nd, 23rd, 27th; October 1st, 2nd, 7th (late afternoon), 12th, 13th, 16th, 23rd, 26th; November 1st (early afternoon).

JOHN LOWE March 24th, 30th; April 4th, 5th*, 6th, 13th, 18th*, 24th*, 25th–29th inclusive; May 6th, 8th, 10th*, 21st, 22nd, 25th, 30th*, 31st; June 4th, 10th, 13th*, 16th*, 25th*, 30th (late afternoon); July 1st, 4th, 5th (late afternoon), 9th, 10th, 14th*, 26th, 30th; August 5th, 9th, 21st, 24th (late afternoon), 28th, 30th (evening), 31st; September 10th (late afternoon), 13th, 17th*, 19th*, 25th (early afternoon); October 1st, 4th*, 6th–8th inclusive, 19th*, 23rd–27th inclusive; November – nil.

RICHARD QUINN March 22nd, 28th–31st inclusive; April 3rd*, 4th, 16th, 22nd, 27th, 30th; May 2nd, 3rd, 12th, 13th, 17th–19th inclusive, 28th, 31st*; June 2nd, 3rd*, 8th, 13th (evening), 16th*, 17th, 22nd (late afternoon), 25th; July 1st (late afternoon),

2nd*, 7th (late afternoon), 10th, 11th, 15th*; August 2nd, 5th, 10th, 16th, 19th, 27th, 28th, 31st; September 2nd*, 8th (evening), 17th, 19th, 25th, 27th, 29th, 30th*; October 3rd, 9th, 19th, 24th, 27th, 30th (evening); November 2nd.

JOHN REID March 25th, 26th (late); April 12th, 13th, 19th, 21st*, 28th; May 1st (early afternoon), 6th, 8th, 9th, 14th, 15th, 22nd (early afternoon); June 11th, 14th, 16th (early afternoon), 30th; July 1st, 6th, 7th, 8th (evening), 10th, 11th, 28th; August 8th, 9th, 13th, 15th–17th inclusive; September 1st, 9th, 13th, 15th, 16th, 25th, 28th, 29th; October 1st, 7th, 20th, 22nd, 25th, 28th, 31st*; November 1st (early afternoon), 2nd.

WALTER SWINBURN March 24th; April 16th, 17th, 18th*, 19th, 24th; May 6th, 7th, 20th, 25th; June 1st, 2nd, 4th, 10th, 21st, 25th, 30th; July 1st, 6th, 9th, 12th, 27th*, 28th; August 2nd, 5th, 9th, 23rd*, 27th, 28th; September 2nd, 7th, 17th, 25th, 27th*; October 4th, 11th*, 16th, 19th, 27th; November 6th (early afternoon).

Trainers for the 1993 Flat Racing Season – Lucky Dates

The following dates could be particularly useful when combined with those previously given for the jockeys.

CLIVE BRITTAIN March 29th (early); April 2nd, 3rd, 6th, 8th, 10th–13th inclusive, 27th; May 9th, 13th, 24th, 27th; June 3rd, 4th, 9th, 10th, 15th, 22nd*; July 11th, 18th–22nd inclusive (22nd*), 24th, 25th; August 11th, 16th, 17th, 18th*, 19th; September 10th*, 11th, 12th, 19th–22nd inclusive, 23rd*, 25th, 26th; October 10th, 11th, 12th*, 13th–15th inclusive; November 1st, 3rd, 4th.

NEVILLE CALLAGHAN March – nil; April 3rd–5th inclusive, 7th, 9th, 28th; May 10th, 13th, 24th, 25th, 27th; June 15th, 16th, 25th, 26th*; July 11th*, 20th, 21st, 23rd, 25th, 26th; August 1st, 11th, 12th, 18th*, 21st; September 5th, 10th–12th inclusive, 22nd, 23rd*, 24th; October 12th*, 13th, 25th, 31st; November 1st.

HENRY CECIL March 31st; April 5th–7th inclusive, 9th, 10th, 28th, 29th; May 11th, 13th, 26th, 27th, 30th, 31st; June 1st, 5th, 11th, 16th, 22nd, 26th; July 1st–3rd inclusive, 12th, 18th, 19th, 22nd–24th inclusive; August 1st, 11th, 18th, 20th, 21st, 31st (late afternoon); September 5th, 11th, 12th, 13th*, 23rd–27th inclusive; October 4th–6th inclusive, 7th*, 8th, 17th, 18th, 31st; November 1st.

GUY HARWOOD March 25th, 31st; April 1st, 2nd, 6th, 23rd; May 9th–11th inclusive, 15th, 16th, 24th*, 27th; June 2nd, 3rd, 9th, 11th, 13th; July 22nd–26th inclusive, 28th; August 1st, 11th*, 17th, 18th, 20th*; September 4th, 10th*, 11th*, 15th, 22nd, 28th; October 6th, 11th, 15th, 17th, 18th, 22nd, 23rd, 28th, 30th; November 2nd.

DICK HERN March 28th; April 2nd*, 8th, 15th, 19th, 26th, 27th*; May 3rd, 8th, 16th, 17th, 21st, 23rd; June 2nd–4th inclusive, 5th*, 9th, 20th, 22nd, 29th; July 3rd, 6th, 22nd, 25th, 26th; August 3rd, 4th, 7th, 8th, 10th, 11th, 22nd, 25th, 27th, 29th; September 5th, 6th, 10th, 11th, 17th, 21st, 26th, 30th; October 1st, 4th, 6th, 15th, 18th, 22nd, 25th; November 3rd, 8th.

BARRY HILLS March 31st; April 1st, 2nd, 14th–16th inclusive, 25th, 27th–29th inclusive; May 1st, 6th–8th inclusive, 14th, 22nd*, 26th, 30th; June 4th, 7th, 12th*, 13th–19th inclusive (16th*), 25th, 30th; July 1st, 3rd, 10th, 13th, 19th*; August 13th*, 14th, 19th, 20th, 29th; September 4th, 9th, 12th–14th inclusive, 25th; October 1st, 4th*, 13th, 14th, 17th, 20th, 28th; November 3rd.

LESTER PIGGOTT March 27th; April 1st, 3rd, 12th, 16th, 22nd, 23rd, 28th; May 1st, 14th, 16th*, 21st, 24th, 29th (late afternoon); June 2nd*, 3rd*, 12th, 17th, 18th, 24th, 25th, 29th; July 2nd*, 9th*, 11th, 23rd (early afternoon), 26th*, 29th, 30th; August 4th*, 5th, 6th*, 12th, 13th (late afternoon), 25th, 26th, 28th (late afternoon), 29th–31st inclusive; September 1st, 2nd, 6th, 7th, 13th, 19th, 24th, 26th; October 9th, 18th, 20th, 26th, 29th; November 3rd.

DAVID O'BRIEN March – nil; April 13th, 14th*, 16th (early afternoon), 17th, 21st, 23rd; May 2nd–4th inclusive, 18th, 30th, 31st; June 1st–10th inclusive (3rd*, 9th*), 12th, 17th–19th inclusive, 26th, 27th, 30th; July 3rd, 7th, 12th, 26th, 30th; August 12th, 20th*, 21st, 30th; September (a good month in general) 2nd, 7th (late afternoon), 22nd, 26th; October 1st, 2nd, 3rd, 18th, 24th (late afternoon), 26th, 29th (late afternoon); November 3rd.

GAVIN PRITCHARD GORDON March 31st; April 1st, 2nd, 23rd; May 1st, 9th, 12th (early afternoon), 13th, 14th, 19th, 20th, 23rd; June 1st, 6th, 9th, 17th, 18th; July 3rd, 12th, 13th, 16th, 24th (late afternoon); August 2nd, 3rd, 7th, 9th–11th inclusive, 16th, 29th, 30th; September 3rd, 6th, 18th, 28th, 30th; October 3rd, 4th, 10th, 13th, 14th; November 3rd.

MICHAEL STOUTE March 24th; April 14th–20th inclusive (16th*, 18th*), 24th, 26th, 27th; May 6th*, 7th, 13th–15th inclusive, 25th, 31st; June 1st, 4th, 5th, 10th, 18th, 19th, 25th; July 1st, 9th, 10th*, 12th, 13th, 27th; August 5th, 12th, 18th, 19th, 22nd, 27th, 28th, 31st; September 6th, 13th (evening), 14th, 25th, 27th; October 3rd–5th inclusive, 19th, 25th, 27th; November – nil.

*These dates are especially good.

The Year In Focus

With lucky Jupiter in an air sign for the majority of this year, you are going to have a personality that could charm serpents, and a mind that is equal to any intellectual task. Your dynamic enthusiasm will take you anywhere you want to go, while your quiet sense of fun will easily gather a crowd.

When it comes to a new year, you have a spontaneous enthusiasm and look forward to it with great anticipation, as much as a small child does to Christmas. However, do not run away with the idea that 1993 will be spectacular. Conversely, neither will it be disastrous. However, at least you will be providentially protected from any serious harm thanks to the presence of Saturn and Jupiter in air signs.

Even so, Uranus and Neptune continue their weary path through Capricorn, creating a certain amount of difficulty for you in matters related to big business, banking, finances etc. Steer clear of these areas if at all possible. If you are seeking backing for your ideas, there could be one or two disappointments ahead. Saturn's placing in Aquarius bodes wonderfully well for the scientific Geminian – you will be making quite an impression on your peers. Concentration will also be increased, and that is good news, especially for the student.

However, avoid getting yourself embroiled in any kind of legal battle. There could be delays and disappointments in this area, and you would be well-advised to settle out of court. It is certainly likely to be one of the most sociable years you have experienced for some time, thanks to the presence of Jupiter in Libra.

You will be expanding your horizons both in leisure-time activities and in friendship circles, where it is very much a case of 'the more the merrier'. Up until November anyway your social calendar will be chock-a-block with dates: full of activity, which is just the way you like it. On the romantic front, in the main most of you will prefer to retain your single status. You are having far too much fun to seriously consider settling down. There are of course exceptions to this during the year, and they are tackled in the following section.

Professionally speaking it should be a spectacular year for the artist, teacher, entertainer, speculator and those involved with animals. For marrieds there could well be an addition to the family. Certainly you and your partner will be broadening your horizons in some area.

Healthwise, naturally there will be the odd occasion when you feel anything but your best, but generally just for once it is a time when you are physically in A1 condition. All in all, then, there is little for you to worry about during the year ahead, so push ahead confidently in the knowledge that the rest of the world is waiting for you.

January

This is a month which professionally favours any members of this sign involved in the stock market, insurance, banking and finance in general. For other Geminians, it is a good time for meetings with people employed in these spheres. Your ruling planet Mercury is in Capricorn between the 3rd and the 20th, which seems to suggest that you will be in a rather sober frame of mind; profound questions about life, death, politics and so on may occupy you more than usual. Not that you will get morbid about such topics, only curious.

Venus at the zenith of your chart gives a helpful boost to those involved in the luxury trades or the arts. It also seems to suggest that you will be combining business with pleasure more than usual. Where romance is concerned opportunities are a little thin on the ground, but this is just as well since you need time to recover from the festive period. Any opportunities which do crop up are likely to be found in connection with work, so you will have more in common with the opposite sex than merely physical attraction.

Mars' position in Cancer is not helpful to your financial state, however. Avoid the sales like the plague, be alert to thieves when in crowds, and refrain from impulsive spending on all sides. You need to conserve cash over the next few months. Healthwise, apart from an occasional hangover and the odd bout of exhaustion you are in A1 condition.

February

February finds you at your most idealistic. Try not to go overboard. In spite of exciting offers and happenings, make an effort to keep one foot on the ground – later on you will be glad you did. It is an especially lucky month for those involved in travel, foreigners, the law and further education. The call of exotic climes will be strong, and many of you will be rushing out to book your summer holiday.

New people enter your life too. Mercury suggests that fresh faces and acquaintances will be revitalizing you and may even lead to romance. Emotionally, Venus in Aries is not the most promising of placings, though it does bring a good deal of fun into your social life directly or indirectly through friends and clubs. You are in a flirty mood, when anyone attempting to pin you down to making a commitment is in for rather a rough ride. You are having far too much fun to even consider it at this moment in time.

Marrieds enjoy themselves, though; communication between you and your partner seems to ease, and you are able to make a fresh start if this is necessary.

Stubbornly, Mars continues to squat in the financial area of your chart, therefore caution is still advised in this area of life. Impulse spending will lead to a good deal of regret, so conserve as much cash as possible until the spring.

March

As always, this is the most ambitious time of the year for you – more so perhaps during 1993, due to the fact that Mercury as well as the Sun is squatting at the zenith of your chart. You will be firing on all four cylinders when it comes to professional affairs. It is a particularly lucky time for those involved in the literary world, or travel, also good for the freelance worker. You will be shining at negotiations and job interviews, making just the right impression.

However, make sure that all this concentration on ambition does not interfere with other areas of your life, particularly if you are married, otherwise there will be some loud objections. Socially, Venus continuing in Aries suggests that once more your social life will be confined to friends and clubs. Home entertaining holds little appeal for you at present, and you want to get away from your base whenever possible.

Financially, Mars in Cancer indicates it is not a time for any kind of investment, gamble, speculation or bargain-hunting; otherwise you are asking for one big kick in the teeth! Health-wise your nerves may play up on occasions, probably due to too many late nights, but otherwise you seem to be providentially protected.

Go after what you want from life during this month, and to your surprise you will discover that you will acquire it more easily and quickly than you would have thought possible.

April

There may be some kind of 'rise' in life during this month. Certainly you will receive a certain amount of recognition, with other people appreciating your past efforts and your future plans.

Much of the emphasis in on the friendship aspect of life, due to the presence of Venus and the Sun in Aries. And when it comes to this area, although you probably know a great many people, even so you have few friends. This is because despite having the personality of a publicist, you are not that easy to get close to. Nevertheless, others will certainly be trying to do so during this month.

On a romantic level, it is friends who make the interesting introductions, so if you are single you should respond to them and their suggestions – you will be glad you did. If you are married, it may be that other people are imposing too much on your spare time, and as a result your relationship could suffer a little. It is up to you to call a halt, as it is likely to be your friends rather than your partner who are creating the problem.

Financially, you will be glad to hear that Mars will finally move out of the financial area of your chart very late in the month. In the meantime, then, this continues to be a time for caution and prudence, when get-rich-quick schemes should be avoided like the plague. Shop only for essentials too. At the present time there is no such thing as a so-called bargain.

Healthwise, once more there is little to hold you back; you are full of vitality, enthusiasm and energy. A reasonably good month provided you are your usual opportunist self.

May

After the hurly-burly of recent months, May could initially seem to be a quite time. Certainly during the early part of the month you are more reclusive and happy to spend time on your own. It appears that you have some world-shattering decisions to make, and you may withdraw from your usual circle of friends at least for a while.

It is certainly a great time for those involved in research or behind-the-scenes activity. However, your mood actually changes when the Sun enters your sign on the 21st. Once this happens you shake off the reclusive mood and are rushing around like a maniac trying to make up for lost time. Late in the month will be a favourable time for freelance work, those employed in the literary world or in travel.

There are plenty of new people entering your life and this proves to be extremely stimulating. Romantically, friends may make some interesting introductions, but it is not a serious time and the word 'commitment' is one you will obliterate from your vocabulary.

Luckily Mars has now moved out of the financial area of your chart, so you can finally begin to make some progress in this direction. Any opportunities that crop up at this time should be seriously considered, but do some investigating before making any kind of promise or commitment.

Mars' placing into Leo suggests that you should be more than usually watchful when on the roads. Obey traffic regulations too, and be especially careful where you park the car. Carelessness in this area could prove to be expensive. Healthwise, apart from the likelihood of a minor prang on the road you remain in fine fettle.

June

This is of course your month – the time of the year when you are at your most confident, enthusiastic and pushy. It is obviously extremely good for the freelance worker, the employer or anyone who feels ready to carve out their own destiny. The Geminian involved in the theatre or the entertainments world should be receiving some good news too. There is more action if this applies to you, and a little less 'resting'.

Your ruling planet Mercury enters the financial area of your chart on the 2nd, so much of your energy at this time will be concentrated on boosting your resources. Just for once you may be reluctant to spend and may even be making provision for the future. Make the most of this placing, it does not often occur. Generally speaking you are an absolute menace when it comes to financial matters.

Romantically, the most enjoyable time of the month is during the first week; after this it is likely that you could become detrimentally involved with the opposite sex. Maybe someone is not being 100 per cent honest with you. So check out everything you are told and do not give your heart away to the first person you meet or there could be big trouble from which you will emerge bruised and bleeding.

Healthwise, Mars continues in Leo, so it is necessary to be a little watchful when on the roads. This pitfall aside, the month should be a relatively fit time.

July

July should be a relatively happy month, so hopefully you have booked your holiday now. If so, there should be few complications – maybe some minor delays, but nothing too awful. Venus is in your sign, therefore you are at your most sociable and romantic – so much so that time spent on your own will be difficult to fit in as you are in such great demand.

It is a wonderful period of the year if you are considering entering into a professional partnership or getting engaged or married. For the single 'that special someone' could be just over the horizon this month, so keep your eyes peeled – this is one of the rare parts of the year when you might just consider giving up your freedom.

On a professional level it is a great time for the artist and those in the moneyed professions, or for dealings with people in such occupations. You will certainly be wanting your pound of flesh when it comes to money. Generally speaking you are an open-handed person, but not so just now. You will expect fair payment for work done, and will be reluctant to lend money to anyone who is unfortunate enough to ask at this particular stage. Make the most of this month to conserve your resources in order to offset any extravagance from which you will no doubt suffer later in the year.

Mars moves into Virgo this month; things could get a little tense at home on occasions, and it is certainly not a time for attempting to move house. If you are decorating and hoping to tackle improvements yourself, be particularly wary of hot and sharp objects. Do not take on anything you are not qualified to tackle, or minor accidents are a possibility. This aside, it should be a healthy month.

August

On the professional level this is a month which favours those involved in advertising and the media, publishing and buying and selling. It is also good for the Geminian wishing to deal with such people. Any chances to take short trips should be snapped up, as you are in a restless mood – reluctant to spend too much time at home, unable to sit still or concentrate.

Venus' placing in the financial area of your chart can only do good and there will be opportunities for you to swell your bank account – the only trouble is that you may be equally inclined to spend on your appearance or perhaps on the home. Furthermore, there may be a tendency to splash out in an effort to impress other people in your emotional life, but this would be wrong. If others cannot accept you for what you are – a charming, intelligent person – then they are not worth bothering with.

Romantically, this is a time when those already in a relationship fare better. Opportunities for meeting new people come very late in the month, but in the main you are more choosy than usual and so mad passionate affairs are unlikely to get off the launching-pad during August – unless of course you are going on holiday, in which case you will be surrounded by admirers. Relationships, be warned, are likely to be short-lived.

September

If you have been waiting for a while to offload property or move house, this is the month for action. If you are happy where you are, then it is likely that you will be entertaining on the home front more than usual, and time spent alone is likely to be limited. Friends and neighbours pop in quite out of the blue, much to your delight, and bring with them some interesting members of the opposite sex.

Professionally speaking, this September favours those involved with property and the allied trades. It is also good for home workers, who will be at their most creative, and will be rewarded justly for efforts made. If you are intending to take any kind of financial risk, then choose the period around the New Moon which is on the 16th. This is when you can be at your most daring, otherwise you would be wise to conserve for the time being anyway.

Romantically, this is hardly the most exciting month of your life. Your social life is hectic enough, but somehow you are more critical than usual and the opposite sex simply does not measure up to your expectations.

Finally, on the health front you should be hale and hearty – unless you are a sports-person, in which case you should be on the alert for strains and sprains. Do not take chances or be over-zealous; you will pay the price if you do.

October

October promises to be just the kind of month you really enjoy: a time bursting full of fun, romance and enjoyment. You are going to be in great demand, and while fulfilling your social obligations will run into attractive members of the opposite sex who will set your heart racing. However, on no account make any promises, since you are in far too flirty a mood to even consider settling down. But members of the opposite sex may not understand this! If you are married, watch out for flirtatious behaviour, which is likely to get you into trouble with your partner. Think twice before being over-friendly in case other people get the wrong ideas.

Professionally, it is those involved with children, animals, the arts or speculation who will be the most successful. Financially speaking, around mid-month you may gain through a calculated risk. But the important word here is 'calculated', for rash gambling will not benefit you at all.

Healthwise Mars and Mercury enter Scorpio, therefore you will be more than usually prone to infections. Stay away from people with 'autumn snuffles'. Furthermore, ensure that you obtain sufficient rest, or those Gemini nerves will be playing you up on occasions. October looks to be an interesting and thoroughly enjoyable month: you do not want to miss it because you are laid up in bed, alone except for some irritating germs.

November

In November there are no fewer than five planets in Scorpio, the area of your life devoted to work and work colleagues. Therefore, it looks as if this is likely to be a 'nose-to-the-grindstone' month. However, it will be a particularly kind one for those involved in the service industries, and good too for Geminians wishing to hire the services of other people – you will certainly get good value for money.

No matter how hale and hearty you are, this is just the month for attending to dental or health problems, so arrange for check-ups now. It is also an ideal time for adopting a new diet or health regime, especially if you are feeling unfit or out of sorts. Mars enters your opposition on the 9th, regrettably making you accident-prone, especially where hot or sharp objects are concerned. Be especially careful in the bathroom and kitchen, and on no account take chances on the road.

Relationships with colleagues will be on the up and up. There-fore do not be too independent, but be ready to cooperate and even seek support when necessary.

Romantically, this is hardly the most exciting month in your life Any encounters that do occur are likely to be in connection with work. You may be temporarily infatuated with a colleague, but the relationship does not appear to be going anywhere so do not pin your hopes on it too much. Clearly then it is the marrieds who fare the best this November.

Financially, there may be some good news for you around the 13th. All in all, a so-so month.

December

Jupiter is now firmly entrenched in Scorpio and your relation-ships with colleagues continue to be on the up-and-up. Further-more, those of you who have been feeling under the weather for some time may experience a vast improvement in your physical condition. There is so much emphasis in your opposition that it is a time when you must be prepared to cooperate and support other people; you simply cannot go off at a tangent in your usual Gemini fashion.

It is certainly a great time for those who are professional managers or agents, or in professional partnerships. Romanti-cally, there is a rosy glow over all existing relationships, and past differences are swept to one side. For the single, this is one of those rare periods in the year when you just might meet 'that special someone' who could positively sweep you off your feet. Marrieds certainly draw closer at this time and feel more able to share their innermost feelings with their partners.

Mars moves into Capricorn during December, advising you against meetings with officialdom, bureaucrats or even the bank manager. Just for once you will not be able to sweet-talk such people, so do not even try. Financially speaking, the best time for any important moves is around the 13th. There may be a fresh source of income for you at this stage.

The Christmas period itself is a little disappointing on Christmas Day, but on Boxing Day the Moon enters your sign and you have the time of your life. As the year draws to a close, on reflection it is likely that you will decide that 1993 was an important year in your development. Happy New Year!

Day-by-day Horoscopes

January

1st – With the Moon in Aries, it is likely that you will carry on your New Year celebrations longer than most people. Friends insist on your company and you are happy to oblige.

2nd – People you meet today will quite inadvertently instil in you a fresh objective or ambition. Constant activity makes it difficult for you to relax.

3rd – Mercury moves into Capricorn, therefore over the next few weeks contracts connected with big business such as the Stock Exchange, insurance and banking will be all important. A good time too for Geminians involved in such occupations.

4th – Venus moves into Pisces, and because of this the creative Geminian can expect considerable success. Clarify your ideas and present them on paper – they are likely to be well received.

5th – With the current position of Venus, it is likely that much socializing will be connected with your professional life. Romance could very well leave the launching-pad through professional affairs, although the marrieds will need to watch out for flirty behaviour.

6th – The Moon in your sign suggests that there is no reason why you should not be enjoying the limelight and in a position to push ahead with all self-interests.

7th – Do not allow other people to interfere with your plans, but stick to what you had intended to do throughout the day. This afternoon is a good time for dealing with bureaucracy.

8th – Today is the Full Moon and it occurs in Cancer, therefore you must guard against mislaying possession. Be tactful and charming at work as there is the slight possibility of a loss of income. Perhaps a contract has reached a conclusion and is up for renewal.

9th – Circumstances beyond your control will affect your day and you will have to fit in with whatever occurs. Try to keep in the mainstream of events, as there are opportunities for fun and pleasure.

10th – The Moon in Leo keeps you on the go. It is a great day for visits and short trips; you should be prepared to travel further for the sake of pleasure or romance.

11th – Give older people the benefit of the doubt, otherwise you could find yourself in trouble. Do not seek confrontation with anybody. 'Keep yourself to yourself' would seem to be the motto of the day.

12th – Make the most of a quiet day by catching up on all those jobs you have been meaning to complete for some time. All forms of communication are highlighted, so make telephone calls and write letters.

13th – Work colleagues will be out to hinder you and you will have difficulty in getting away from them. Try to complete all routine work early in the day, as a more challenging opportunity comes later.

14th – Those younger than yourself will have some excellent ideas on how to improve your income. Listen carefully to what they say. This is not the best day of the week for tackling superiors, however.

15th – Associates and colleagues seem determined to confuse you over a work matter; try to avoid them wherever practical. If attending interviews or business discussions, allow other people to do the talking.

16th – Not a good day for finances or personal possessions. Keep a close eye on all valuables, as they are likely to disappear through neglect or theft. Also make certain the home is secure before leaving.

17th – A rather tiring day when you will find your energy level letting you down when you most need it. Try to avoid making elementary mistakes which could be difficult to rectify.

18th – Someone will come into your life who either is foreign or has a foreign-sounding name. This person could become a friend or romantic partner. The evening is a good time for accepting invitations.

19th – Make certain your plans are not too complicated, or you could find yourself at a loose end through having arrangements cancelled. Courtesy calls are not advised, as other people wish to be on their own.

20th – Your ruling planet Mercury moves into Aquarius, therefore all matters related to foreign affairs, education or the law are well-starred. Further, it is likely that there is an opportunity to go on a long-distance trip. If so, take advantage.

21st – A member of the opposite sex will be attracted to you, but not necessarily on a romantic level. Help will also come from this direction. There will be a minor upset to career plans.

22nd – This is New Moon day, and it falls in Aquarius. If you have a loved one abroad, you will certainly be hearing from them. Those involved with litigation would be wise to consider settling out of court.

23rd – Try not to be too hard on people who do not come up to your expectations in all respects. They may hinder you, but could also do with your assistance. This evening is a good time for family get-togethers.

24th – The further you get away from your home base today, the better. You are in one of your restless moods, and will be revitalized by fresh places and new locations.

25th – Anyone connected with outdoor activities will have an excellent day, especially where teamwork is involved. If working in or around the home, enlist the help of friends or family.

26th – Keep your options open as there are some good invitations coming your way. Accept those which allow you to mix business with pleasure, or those proffered by workmates.

27th – Be careful when dealing with strangers, as they will try to pull the wool over your eyes – especially tradespeople with whom you are unfamiliar. Check your change carefully after paying for purchases.

28th – Try to sort out a family problem which has become pressing. Friends are able to offer good advice, but you should not accept any financial help.

29th – Take care of work around the home. Electrical appliances are likely to go haywire, but do not attempt any do-it-yourself repairs, as this could lead to more problems. For others it is a day of ups and downs.

30th – Older people could be out to give you a hard time. Try to go along with their plans rather than rub them up the wrong way. This afternoon is a good time for contacting people who have been elusive.

31st – The month goes out on a high note, and you seem to find the solution to a pressing financial problem. Not a day for being too adventurous socially – you will prefer to sit quietly at home.

February

1st – The fact that the Moon is in your sign at the beginning of the month seems to bode well. However, your nervous energy is on the rampage and concentration will be difficult.

2nd – A very good time for all those involved in sporting or other outdoor activities. Others should get out of the home today in order to find maximum entertainment.

3rd – Today Venus moves into Aries, throwing a rosy glow over friendship and club activities. Other people may be making some interesting romantic introductions; do not be too proud.

4th – Domestic matters will be running smoothly and you will be feeling well able to cope with jobs in hand. A good day for approaching colleagues for favours.

5th – Business discussions are bound to be fruitful. Those in a partnership or who earn a living as freelance workers will have an excellent day. You may need to rest up this evening, though.

6th – Today is Full Moon day, and it occurs in Leo: a warning, if ever there was one, to take extra care when on the roads. If anyone is going to meet an idiot behind a wheel, it is likely to be you, so be careful.

7th – You may have to make compromises where family matters are under discussion. A new financial budget may need to be worked out with the co-operation of loved ones and family members.

8th – Mercury moves into Pisces at the zenith of your chart, which is particularly good news for those involved with travel, the literary world or communications. Minor changes are expected for other Geminians.

9th – Do not stay around the house any longer than is absolutely necessary – you are in an adventurous mood, and will become bored and restless at home. Seek out friends who like to experiment, and generally keep yourself busy.

10th – Matters which concern you on a personal level should be dealt with today. This is a good time for having family discussions. The opinions of others are bound to differ from your own.

11th – A very good day for all those wishing to go into business on their own account. Seek professional advice whenever you feel it necessary to lessen the risk of mistakes.

12th – Those out and about are likely to find themselves in something of a muddle around midday. Do not take the advice or directions of others – you could be misled if you do.

13th – Disruptions within the domestic scene will upset you and cause preoccupation; because of this, errors are likely. Try to pay close attention to the job in hand. Avoid do-it-yourself repairs.

14th – The Moon in your opposition suggests that the day's activities are likely to be in the hands of other people, and you should be generously prepared to go along with them.

15th – Heavy domestic expenditure will give you cause for concern, so try to keep expenses as low as possible. This evening appears to be a time for domestic wrangling.

16th – The moon moves into Capricorn, therefore you need to proceed very carefully when dealing with those in big business, such as bureaucrats, officials, the Stock Exchange or your bank manager. Misunderstandings will crop up without warning.

17th – Courtesy calls on business contacts and relatives will run far from smoothly, so it would be better to shelve visits until a more favourable time. Domestic problems are likely to be resolved this evening.

18th – Good opportunities are there for the taking, but you need to be alert. Keep your eyes and ears open whenever you are in the company of superiors or older colleagues.

19th – Do not try to rush through jobs of a routine nature as errors are likely to occur which will hold you up for the rest of the day. Care should be taken in all areas.

20th – A better day for putting financial plans into operation; those seeking loans should be lucky. Also, the unemployed will hear some encouraging news this afternoon.

21st – This is the day of the New Moon and it occurs at the zenith of your chart. Such a placing bodes well for those attending job interviews. Others will receive news of promotion or change – either way it is a progressive time.

22nd – Rely on your own resources today and accept help from nobody. You are far better equipped to deal with routine matters when working under your own steam.

23rd – A good day for all those travelling, since hindrances and delays will be non-existent. Parents will find children difficult to handle throughout the day, and will need patience.

24th – A quiet day when you will be able to catch up on personal matters such as correspondence etc. This evening could become somewhat traumatic because of the intervention of in-laws.

25th – Older work colleagues will need to be handled with tact and diplomacy in order to avoid conflict and confrontation. This afternoon will be their most irritable time.

26th – Before giving any assistance to others, make certain that you have your own work well in hand. Delays will lead to complications, which may be difficult to rectify.

27th – A good day for making contact with influential people at home and abroad. Foreigners are likely to feature in the day's events. This evening is a time for family get-togethers.

28th – Your ruling planet Mercury moves into retrograde action, therefore progress is likely to be of the one-step-forward, two-steps-back variety for a little while and you will need considerable patience – not your strong suit.

March

1st – Do not allow other people to deflect you from your main target, but push ahead with confidence. Family and friends will involve you in a financial outlay this afternoon.

2nd – A good day for all who are out and about or involved in sporting activities. Those at home will become restless and bored very easily. Invitations for this evening should be accepted. The problems of children will put parents on the spot.

3rd – Those with career problems should give some thought to considering their position. You will certainly need some time to yourself at some point during the day. A good time for solving partnership problems.

4th – Circumstances beyond your control will make for an interesting but muddled day. Try to stick to a routine pattern wherever possible. Avoid unnecessary expense this evening.

5th – A day when colleagues will make life difficult for many, but you should be able to take this in your stride. Financial matters come in for discussion with a marriage partner.

6th – Pay attention to warning signs given out by your body; minor health problems should not be neglected. This afternoon is a good time for dealing with officialdom.

7th – Travel arrangements may have to be postponed due to the incapacity of a relative or loved one. Financial outlay could be heavier than usual this evening.

8th – This is Full Moon day and it occurs in Virgo , which suggests the end of a minor cycle in connection with domestic or property affairs. Not a time for beginning anything new – and that includes relationships.

9th – All forms of outdoor activity are well-starred, so get out and about as much as possible. Relatives could prove rather irritating this evening – so steer clear.

10th – Courtesy calls should be made early in the day, as you will not feel like persuading or coaxing other people during the afternoon. Catch up on personal matters including telephone calls and correspondence this evening.

11th – Minor health problems should have eased and you will be more or less up to scratch. Tackle jobs that are routine and make no important decisions until further notice.

12th – The moon moves into Scorpio today. On the one hand the atmosphere at work and your relationships with colleagues will improve. Conversely, health is likely to suffer through your own over-indulgence during the next few weeks.

13th – Check your mail this morning – you could be missing something of importance. This afternoon is the best time for getting on the phone and making arrangements with friends or relatives.

14th – Make decisions today and stick to them; those around you may be trying to throw you off-course. This evening is a time for dealing with domestic problems.

15th – Romances begun this week stand a fair chance of success, but do not make any promises you feel unable to keep. This evening is a time to be spent within the family circle.

16th – Travel arrangements which have been made on your behalf will come under scrutiny, and you may have to change them to suit your movements. Neighbours could give you problems this afternoon.

17th – Plan a quiet day at work. You are in an erratic frame of mind and experience many changes of mood, so it is best to avoid intricate tasks. Further, stay clear of awkward people this evening.

18th – Jointly-held finances come under discussion, and some changes will have to be made. Those with joint finances at risk will be in danger of loss, so pull out wherever possible.

19th – Extra responsibility could come your way, due to family problems. Try to take everything in your stride. This afternoon will be taken up with family and personal matters.

20th – Minor health problems caused through stress could mar your day. Irritability will be your main problem. Friends and relatives will be giving you a wide berth.

21st – Other people will frustrate and anger you during the day due to their unpredictable behaviour. Do not confront them directly – you could come off worst in any argument.

22nd – You will need all your energy today as routine work will take on a new meaning; moreover, extra responsibility could come your way. Make all long-distance calls early in the day.

23rd – Today is the day of the New Moon, and it falls in Aries; this suggests that in the near future you will be introduced to a fresh circle of friends, and you may also be joining a new club.

24th – Mercury has finally decided to resume forward action, therefore at last you can begin to make some progress. Frustrations of the past are swept out of the way.

25th – A settled home life will make you that much more determined to succeed at work. Career matters can be discussed with superiors, who should give you some good advice.

26th – You will be engrossed in what is going on around you today – so much so that you could leave important work unfinished. Try not to allow this to occur.

27th – Curb expansive behaviour and do not be too extravagant when buying household items. This afternoon is an ideal time for business meetings and discussions.

28th – Keep yourself to yourself and do not become involved in the problems of colleagues and/or neighbours. Much of your time this evening will be taken up with family matters.

29th – Nerves could be a problem, but you should be able to cope. Colleagues will come to your assistance should you require them to do so. Do not be backward in asking for help.

30th – Take advantage of any opportunities that present themselves today – you could make some extra cash. Younger people have some good ideas for entertaining this evening.

31st – A good day for romance, and any relationships begun today stand a fair chance of lasting. Marrieds will find partners cooperative and willing to go along with financial plans.

April

1st – You may find other people a trifle irritating in their behaviour. Plan the day according to your own ideas – this is not a time to rely on others.

2nd – Give careful consideration to financial offers which come your way. You may be asked to participate in something which is not entirely above-board.

3rd – Single Geminians will probably have their mind on romance and/or friendship, rather than anything more serious. Marrieds too are out to enjoy themselves, and will draw closer as a result.

4th – Changes that are taking place in your personal life may not work out as you had hoped. Do not become irritated or bitter if someone is making greater progress than you are.

5th – You have little or no control over conditions at home or at work at present, and will have to remain flexible in order to get through the next week or so.

6th – This is the day of the Full Moon, and it occurs in Libra. Therefore it is likely that something you have been looking forward to may be cancelled at the last moment. Not a good time for romance – it could bite the dust.

7th – If you are out and about today, do not put your trust in strangers – you could be misled or misdirected. Those travelling will find that minor hitches spoil well-laid plans. Arrange a relaxing evening.

8th – Today is likely to be marred by minor accidents such as cuts, bruises and burns. Take extra care when handling hot and sharp instruments or tools, and avoid strenuous pastimes.

9th – A very good day for sorting out your domestic problems, as partners will be cooperative and understanding. Singles may not be so lucky, and a relationship could come to an end.

10th – Extra responsibility could come your way due to the incapacitation of a relative or loved one. Make the most of the situation to show how deeply you feel about them. Neighbours may also come to the rescue.

11th – The Moon is in your opposition today, therefore there is little point in expecting to get your own way. It will become necessary for you to consider the ideas and feelings of other people more than you usually do.

12th – A day from which you will be able to extract as much as you put in. Do not expect miracles. There are some good opportunities around, but you will have to move speedily in order to catch them.

13th – Clear up all your personal affairs today, including any domestic problems you may have. You will need to compromise with a relative in order to settle an outstanding issue.

14th – Do not be too proud to back down in the face of adversity – you will gain far more by being sensible than stubborn. This evening is the best time for tackling children's problems.

15th – Push ahead with long-term financial plans. You may be thinking of rearranging your household budget; if so, now is an excellent time to do so.

16th – Mercury moves into Aries – this is good news for those who work as part of a team, and there may be a fresh objective.

Other Geminians are likely to be attracted to new people, many of whom will be younger than yourself.

17th – Your day's plans may have to be altered due to events beyond your control. This will be especially upsetting for those who were looking forward to something special. Be adaptable.

18th – While it may be a Sunday, for some reason or other you cannot get work out of your head. Perhaps you have taken home some paperwork in order to catch up.

19th – The Sun moves into Taurus today; therefore you begin a period when you should trust your intuition rather than your grey matter when it comes to solving problems, as it is unbeatable.

20th – Work carried on in and around the home will be most satisfying, and do-it-yourself enthusiasts will have a very pleasant time. Do not try to do too much, however.

21st – This is the day of the New Moon and it occurs in Aries, suggesting that in the very near future you will be introduced into a fresh circle of friends – this could lead to romance.

22nd – While some progress can be made today, it will not be outstanding. Obstacles in your way will be difficult to remove. Colleagues seem to be deliberately unhelpful.

23rd – Venus resumes forward movement, therefore you must take care; for when it comes to the romantic side of life you are in danger of being your own worst enemy. Check out the status of new people who come on the scene: someone may be out to deceive you.

24th – Neptune goes into retrograde action, and because of this work and career problems could become unbelievably muddled and complicated over the next few weeks.

25th – A good day for getting as far away from home as is feasible. However, if you are relying on public transport it is likely that delays and cancellations will ruin your plans.

26h – A day when misunderstandings will lead to disappointment. Double-check all arrangements, especially if they have been made by someone else on your behalf. The Moon in your sign means that you will be at your most confident.

27th – Those connected with sport in any way will have a satisfying and, in some cases, profitable day. This does not mean, however, that gamblers should go crazy; keep your stakes small.

28th – Visit business contacts and friends today before they complain about your ignoring them. You may even enjoy yourself as well as making a profit.

29th – A day when older colleagues will be willing to help out in return for small favours. Only grant these if you really need their assistance and/or advice, however.

30th – The month goes out on a good note. Partnership and domestic problems appear to be easing, and you are feeling more settled than you have done for some time.

May

1st – Do not run away with the idea that others are lending a helping hand because they like you – they are after something! Check all motives when any assistance is offered.

2nd – Do not depend on other people, as they will only make your life difficult. Rely on your own intuition and judgement, make your decisions and stick to them, and then you cannot go wrong.

3rd – A day when all arrangements should be double-checked, since what has been fixed on your behalf may fall through. Those travelling are also in for a few nasty shocks.

4th – Your ruling planet Mercury moves into Taurus. This suggests that over the next couple of weeks you should put away the active grey matter and rely on your strong intuitions: they will serve you well.

5th – Relatives will make pleasant company this evening, so now is the time to pay those neglected visits. Geminians travelling under their own steam will experience delays.

6th – This is the day of the Full Moon, and it occurs in Scorpio. Therefore it is not a time for crossing swords with colleagues – rather, spend your time putting the finishing touches to outstanding work.

7th – Those who have professional interests in the Stock Exchange, insurance etc. can expect a profitable day. Others will find that this is a good time for planning cash moves.

8th – Not the best day of the week for getting together with friends; they will be difficult to locate, and when you do catch up with them you will not find their company particularly congenial.

9th – Older relatives can help you with a personal matter, so seek their help and advice. You may have to give something in exchange. Calls made to romantic partners tonight will be confused.

10th – Younger people have a harrowing effect upon you, so steer clear of them whenever possible. This evening is a good time for mixing business with pleasure.

11th – Those connected with sporting activities will find themselves with a small celebration on their hands. Financial rewards can also be expected.

12th – A good time for clearing out the house. Something of value which has been hidden may well turn up. Give thought and consideration to the problems of youngsters.

13th – A good note on which to begin the weekend, as finances receive a boost. New ways of earning extra cash will also be made clear to you. A chance to receive a rise in salary is in the air.

14th – This Friday a cloud of depression which has been hanging around for a little while will be lifted, and you will feel like making progress. Put short-term plans into operation.

15th – A good day for those who like to take a financial risk; gamblers can put spare cash at stake. This afternoon is the best time for pinning down an elusive friend or lover.

16th – If you are in and around the home then take care with electrical appliances; there may be a small risk here. Do-it-yourself repairs are not recommended – call in the professionals wherever necessary.

17th – Colleagues will be irritable and argumentative, therefore steer clear of them and do not push for confrontation. This evening is a good time for dealing with family problems.

18th – Your ruler Mercury moves into your own sign and enlivens your own entire personality. Mentally you are razor-sharp, and it will take a clever person to pull one over on you. A good time for those involved with the media, travelling or sales.

19th – Plan a quiet day in order to recharge your batteries. This afternoon is a great time for putting the finishing touches to a purely personal matter. A quiet drink at your local pub should be the most energetic thing you do this evening.

20th – If your job is connected with abroad, and foreigners in particular, make sure your aggressive instincts do not lead you into trouble. Curb your temper.

21st – A good day for all those working from home; some welcome news comes to you through the mail. This afternoon should be spent in catching up on neglected routine matters.

22nd – This is the middle of the New Moon period and it falls in your sign. Therefore you can expect a fresh beginning at some point in the very near future.

23rd – The big astrological news is that Saturn has moved into Pisces. Therefore it is likely that where career matters are concerned you will be gaining some heavy responsibility – but also extra reward.

24th – Those working on their own behalf will have difficulty in raising cash for a new idea. You will have to plod on as usual for a few more weeks before making any progress.

25th – Get out and about if you wish to have an enjoyable day – there is little to be gained by sitting around at home. This is not the best time for home entertaining.

26th – Emergency calls on older relatives or work contacts will leave you feeling depressed. Try to make them early in the day so as to give yourself a chance to revive later.

27th – Make other people aware of your ambitious aims; they will help you to achieve your goals if they are in the know. Marriage partners are loving and understanding.

28th – Give older colleagues a wide berth this morning, as they will not be in the best of moods. Housewives will probably be having trouble with neighbours this afternoon.

29th – A good day for completing jobs around the home which have been hanging fire for some while now. This afternoon is great for beginning anything new – and that includes relationships. Make some plans of a challenging nature.

30th – Those who are planning a journey ought to reconsider their plans, since delays will cause difficulties and disappointments. It would be better to stay close to your home or work base.

31st – The month goes out on a good note financially; many of you will receive cash windfalls of some description. This evening is a favourable time for having a small gamble.

June

1st – Partners and loved ones may be giving you cause for suspicion. Find out what is going on before making accusations you cannot retract. You will have to choose between friends.

2nd – Mercury moves into the financial area of life. This means that over the next few weeks it is likely that you will be gaining from travel, new projects and contracts. Fresh people who enter your life will be lucky.

3rd – The Moon is in Scorpio, therefore now is a great time for smoothing out differences with colleagues. There also may be some new members of the staff – if so, extend a hand of friendship.

4th – This is the day of the Full Moon and it occurs in your opposition. This seems to suggest that feelings which have been boiling beneath the surface finally rise, much to your surprise. You could be in for something of a shock.

5th – No point in attempting to go off at a tangent today; you will need to consider other people's feelings whether you like it or not. Stifle your independent soul, then, for the time being.

6th – Venus moves into Taurus. Be warned that when it comes to a romantic affair you should dig around in the background of things, as other people will not be completely open and candid with you. You could be your own worst enemy in this respect.

7th – There are people around you who are willing to give assistance in return for favours, but choose your associates carefully. This afternoon is best for long-distance communication.

8th – A good day for all those about to embark on protracted journeys or holidays abroad. Arrangements will work out as planned, and there is little to bother you.

9th – The call of the outdoors will be difficult to resist, and many of you will be visiting places as yet unseen. For those who are working this may be difficult, but try to find excuses to get out even if it is only for a few moments. An adventurous day.

10th – You should be taking an interest in what is going on around you – this is the way to pick up on some useful ideas. Cash can be made by those who are willing to take a few risks.

11th – Those seeking your advice could be approaching the wrong person. Your judgement is not all it should be at present. Avoid counselling others, therefore.

12th – The Moon is at the zenith of your chart this Saturday, which makes it difficult for you to relax. Seek out the company of those who really know how to make you laugh and enjoy yourself.

13th – The Moon in Aries suggests that you could not spend the day better than getting in touch with friends, who will be in fine humour. Someone new you meet sets you off on a fresh hobby or interest.

14th – You really have some excellent ideas today, but now is not the right time to put them into action so shelve them until a later date. This evening is a good time for home entertaining.

15th – A very good day for all matters concerning your personal relationships. Romantic encounters are likely, although the object of your desires could be much younger than yourself.

16th – Older relatives will be pleased to see you today, so make courtesy calls now. Travel arrangements may go awry, so ensure that contacts are aware of where and when they are meeting you.

17th – Although the financial scene is looking up you will need to control your expenditure for some time to come. Do not put cash at risk, as this is not a good time for investments.

18th – Colleagues will be helpful and this is a good time to become involved in a partnership of some description. Those around you will be loving and cooperative.

19th – The Moon is in your sign today, therefore it is just the appropriate moment for pushing yourself and your interests to the fore with confidence.

20th – Today is the day of the New Moon, and it falls in the financial area of your chart. Therefore, in the near future you can expect a fresh source of income. A good time for new beginnings, too.

21st – Do not allow other people to steer you away from your main goal; you have much to gain through forging ahead now. Make loved ones aware of your future ambitions.

22nd – Give friends the benefit of the doubt if differences of opinion arise, otherwise arguments and bad feelings will ensue. Keep children occupied this afternoon.

23rd – Mars moves into Virgo today. This is the domestic and property area of life, therefore you can expect a certain amount of tension and strain to develop over the next few weeks.

24th – There is little to be gained from confrontations with colleagues – it would be better to work together. All joint efforts will be rewarded.

25th – Those with whom you are dealing on a professional basis may be difficult to pin down, and decisions you are awaiting will not be forthcoming.

26th – Health should be at its peak, and you are feeling on top of everything. Avoid the temptation to be over-confident, as you could upset those around you.

27th – There will be opportunities around for you to earn some extra cash in the near future, probably due to the ideas of a friend, relative or partner. Lay down your plans, but do not invest any money as yet.

28th – Those who are carrying out work on your behalf – such as tradespeople, delegates and so on – should be checked from time to time, as mistakes are likely.

29th – A good day for all open-air activities. Those who are homebound at present will become restless and bored. This is a favourable time for mixing business with pleasure.

30th – Today there will be plenty of opportunities to meet interesting members of the opposite sex. The single can take romantic advantage of this – but marrieds should not do so!

July

1st – The Moon is in your opposition, so do not be surprised if other people are less than cooperative. It is very much a time for going all out on your own. Expect a certain restlessness within all relationships.

2nd – Saturn has decided to go into retrograde action. This means that all matters related to big business such as finance, banking, insurance etc. are prone to complication; therefore you will need to proceed carefully in these areas.

3rd – This is Full Moon day – not a time to push your luck where officials or bureaucrats are concerned. Be warned that if you break traffic regulations, you are the one who is likely to get caught.

4th – There will be an opportunity for you to attend a party, probably at a foreigner's house, and although initially you may not feel like doing so, later on you perk up and decide to go along. You will be glad you did.

5th – Partnership financial affairs will fare better today. This is a good time for putting joint finances at risk. There are times for celebration throughout the day.

6th – Venus moves into your sign, therefore you are at your most attractive, both physically and mentally. If you are single, you are bound to meet someone important during the next few weeks. It is a great time for engagements and marriages.

7th – Married partners will be in a fun-loving mood. It would be best to go along with them, as things could change during the coming week when they become more introverted and boring.

8th – Not the best day of the week for signing any official documents or contracts. Steer clear of making hard and fast decisions regarding financial matters.

9th – You are heading for a bout of depression, probably brought about by your domestic scene. Try to work through it and keep yourself occupied.

10th – Make your social plans early in the day, and stick to them rigidly. You will be badgered by time-wasters and you will have to show them the door.

11th – Make the most of changes that are taking place in your personal life. You will find that if you remain flexible you will get a great deal of enjoyment from the day's events.

12th – Those around you are willing to grant favours as long as you commit yourself to them. This is not the time to be beholden to other people, however.

13th – Romance is possible for the single today; a relationship begun now is likely to be long-lived. Friendship matters are also highlighted. All in all, it will be an enjoyable day.

14th – A good day for working in and around the home. Decor changes are likely. This afternoon is a favourable time for having people over for a get-together.

15th – End-of-week blues will probably last for the majority of the day unless you can find yourself a challenging task. Routine work will give you no satisfaction whatsoever. Be adventurous.

16th – Make certain that other people do not steal your lime-light. With the Moon in your sign you can push yourself to the forefront of the day's events; there is nothing to be gained from taking a back seat.

17th – A good day for presenting new ideas for doing old jobs to your superiors; ingenuity will be appreciated. This afternoon favours those working from home.

18th – Financial problems ideally should be discussed with a professional. The advice of friends may be well-meant, but it is misleading and inaccurate.

19th – This is the day of the New Moon and it falls in the financial area of life. Be on your alert for opportunities. Certainly it is a great day for attending job interviews: you will shine.

20th – Those connected with the sporting side of life will have an excellent day. The organizers will make a profit and the participants can expect great satisfaction.

21st – Plan a quiet time at work; do not attempt to do anything which is out of the ordinary or involves a gamble. This is not a time to be daring, or indulge in strenuous activity. A routine day.

22nd – Beware of overwork. You may have done with depression, but headaches and nervous problems could follow in its wake. This evening is a bad time for home entertaining.

23rd – The Sun moves into Virgo, and in doing so throws the emphasis on home, domesticity and property affairs. Just the right time for house-hunting, or for entertaining important contacts.

24th – This is a good day for those who are travelling. New people you meet will be both exciting and interesting. The more adventurous you are, the better. Anything but a run-of-the-mill time, then.

25th – Go it alone today; other people will not be able to keep up with you, and much time will be wasted. Be ready to accept any last-minute invitations that come your way, as they should prove to be worthwhile.

26th – Finally Mercury has decided to see sense and resume forward action. This means that from now on you will begin to make real progress.

27th – Be on your guard when mixing with people to whom you are not known. Something you say may be turned against you at a later date. Place your trust in friends only.

28th – A good day for travelling, whether short distances or protracted journeys. Those embarking on an annual holiday will have chosen a lucky time.

29th – There is a chance of romance for the single, but care should be taken when making commitments. You may find it difficult to keep your promises later.

30th – This is not a good day to put finances at risk. Other people are trying to get what they can from you. Housewives will probably be cheated at the shops.

31st – Make the most of offers of assistance which come your way – you could do with a spot of help at present. This evening is an excellent time for mixing business with pleasure.

August

1st – If you are sensible you will plan a quiet day. Travelling is unlucky and arduous. No reason, though, why you should not get on the phone and ask a few friends around for a quiet drink.

2nd – This is the day of the Full Moon and it occurs in the financial area of your life. Take care of possessions and ensure that you avoid any kind of financial commitment. A contract may be reaching the end of its duration.

3rd – A good day for all those participating in physical-contact sports, when a minor celebration is likely. An active day for most members of this sign.

4th – Pluto resumes a forward action, therefore any difficulties you may have been experiencing with officialdom or bureaucracy should slowly become a thing of the past. Be open in all of your dealings.

5th – A romantic relationship will deepen and you could find yourself making a strong commitment. Marrieds will be likewise involved. A romantic day all in all.

6th – Work colleagues will offer suggestions on ways to increase your productivity and your income. Look to the past for an answer to a problem which is bothering you at present.

7th – Because the Moon is in Aries this makes it a wonderful weekend for getting together with friends or visiting clubs. New people who enter your life will be stimulating, and there may be romance in the air.

8th – It continues to be a time when you are at your most sociable. People appreciate your company no matter where they may find you. Romance is moderately well-starred but is not likely to be serious.

9th – The Moon is in Taurus, and suggests that you should rely on your instincts instead of your grey matter. Any gut feelings you have in reaction to situations or people will be correct.

10th – Mercury moves into Leo and this bodes well for Geminians involved in advertising, publishing, sales or the media. It is also a good time for making business trips over the next few weeks.

11th – There is a lot of to-ing and fro-ing within your home base today – it looks as if you will be entertaining relatives or friends. Try to keep the expenses down, and avoid going over the top.

12th – Mars moves into Libra, which gingers up all activities and matters related to children, also sports and romance. However, be warned that tension can flare up at any moment within these areas.

13th – Housewives shopping in their own neighbourhoods are likely to find themselves being cheated by tradespeople. Check all change when leaving tills and counters.

14th – If you are travelling today, make certain you are following

72

the right route; time could be wasted by getting yourself lost. Do not rely on strangers for directions, either.

15th – The Moon in Cancer seems to suggest that you are preparing to spend in order to impress – wrong – just be your normal sweet self: if this is not sufficient for others, they are simply not worth bothering with.

16th – The Moon in Leo makes it a great time for taking short trips, bargain-hunting or straightforward shopping. Those waiting for news regarding recent job interviews should be lucky.

17th – The day of the New Moon, and it is likely that you will be changing your mind over an important matter. This is likely to cause a few surprised or shocked faces, but if you are convinced you are in the right, then proceed regardless.

18th – This is the day to spend with close friends and loved ones. Married partners are cooperative and agreeable. Plan a romantic evening if at all possible. Keep work matters routine.

19th – Do not carry confidence too far, otherwise you could end up making yourself very unpopular. Colleagues will be willing to help you out, but not if they are bullied into it.

20th – Keep yourself in the mainstream of events today; you will learn a lot to your advantage. This afternoon is good for putting the finishing touches to a cherished plan.

21st – Listen to what other people have to say – you could learn a lot about current conditions, in both your personal and your professional life. This evening is a likely time for romantic encounters.

22nd – Care should be taken of your health. Nervous problems are likely to cause headaches and psychosomatic illnesses. Try to plan a quiet day if at all possible.

23rd – You will need plenty of stamina to get you through the day, but the jobs you set yourself will be disagreeable. Try to find intellectual challenges to stimulate your interest.

24th – Make the most of any help offered to you today. Those who are decorating or beautifying their surroundings will benefit from the advice of people younger than themselves.

25th – You will have to devote much of your day to the needs of elderly relatives, since you will be at their beck and call. A few anxious moments will be spent on their behalf.

26th – Mercury moves into Virgo, gingering up the activity at home. If you are involved in buying or selling a house, then a contract will come through in the very near future. Surprise visitors can be expected.

27th – Other people will be at your command, and this is a great time to get what you want from them. Favours will not need to be asked for – they will be given, anyway.

28th – Venus moves into Leo, making this a wonderful time for travelling; so if you are setting off on your annual holiday, you have chosen a good time for doing so. Those at home are prone to exciting brief encounters.

29th – Get as far away as possible from your home base. You are in an adventurous mood, and need some excitement and unfamiliar faces to stimulate you.

30th – A good day for signing official documents and those that are financially binding. New contracts made today will be beneficial to you in the future.

31st – Visitors coming to see you today will be delayed, and you will have to change your plans at the last moment. However, your day should still be filled with enjoyment.

September

1st – This is Full Moon day, and it occurs at the zenith of your chart. Tread very carefully, then, as changes are likely on the professional front and you do not want one of them to be you! Try to put finishing touches to existing work; begin nothing new.

2nd – Give all colleagues a wide berth as they are not seeing eye to eye with you at present. You will have to make concessions in order to regain their companionship.

3rd – Relatives will have some effect on the day's events, probably due to the fact that they are pressing you for favours of some description. Do not loan cash to them.

4th – Some changes which are taking place around you will affect you indirectly. A colleague is either retiring or resigning, and you could be asked to step into his/her shoes.

5th – Not a time for gadding around – you need to take it easy and rest up. Force yourself to wind down and really let go, or your health could be affected in the near future.

6th – Do not make promises that you feel you will be unable to keep in future. This applies especially to those involved in heavy romance. Others will let friends down at some point.

7th – Partners are very romantic today and you could be in for a few nice surprises – the marrieds especially. This evening is an excellent time for the single to enter into a liaison.

8th – Those involved in work around the home will not be feeling up to it. Try to keep your mind on the job, and do not tackle anything that is unfamiliar or dangerous.

9th – Today favours your getting things under way, be they personal or business concerns. Those involved in financial matters should push ahead. This is an extremely profitable day.

10th – Care should be taken when dealing with officials of any description – they could make life difficult if you are not nice to them, so be charming and pleasant.

11th – Mercury moves into Libra. From now on it is likely to be mental rather than physical hobbies and interests that stimulate you. For the creative Gemini, a contract seems to be just over the horizon.

12th – This is a day when the Moon is in Cancer, and you will be inclined to spend in order to impress other people – not a good idea, for you really cannot afford it at present. Besides, they should like you for what you are.

13th – Domestic matters have a beneficial effect on your day. Partners are particularly loving at present, and you will be feeling expansive and happy.

14th – A good day for embarking on a period of self-improvement, an image change or new hairstyle. Many of you will be considering enrolment in evening classes and becoming involved in specialized clubs and associations.

15th – Give partners all the help they ask for around the home today. Joint efforts are likely to be more successful than activities undertaken alone. This evening is a good time for romance.

16th – Be careful when handing out advice today. Your judgement is not all that it should be, and you could make things worse instead of better. Financial losses are likely this evening.

17th – Be prepared to work harder than usual, after a slow start to the day. Interruptions and hindrances beyond your control will make this a frustrating time.

18th – Expect the unexpected in your domestic surroundings. Housewives will find appliances blowing up on them, and chaos will rule. Those at home will experience delays at every turn.

19th – Those travelling today should make certain of their routes; strangers will be deliberately misleading when giving directions. All in all, this could be a wasted day.

20th – Some people around you are trying to get the better of you. If you are involved in arguments, give way rather than participate in a battle to the end.

21st – Get all those niggling jobs around the home cleared up and out of the way. Tasks which are left to hang fire now will only deteriorate as time progresses.

22nd – Venus moves into Virgo. This suggests that you are about to enter a phase when you will be involved in increased home entertaining, or beautifying your home. Certainly a pleasant period domestically.

23rd – The Sun moves into Libra, and with this you start the fun-loving and light-hearted part of the year. Good too for those professionally involved in speculation, creativity, animals and the arts.

24th – Someone in your household is spending more than they should be; discover the culprit and have words. You may need to re-budget in order to get things back on an even keel.

25th – A favourable day for getting things moving. There is plenty to do around the home, but you should be able to cope and still have time and energy left over for fun. This evening is a good time for pinning down would-be lovers.

26th – A decision you have been waiting for in your personal life is likely to come through today. Others will find that promises made some time ago are finally kept.

27th – Those involved in strenuous activity are likely to do themselves a minor injury – take care. This will be a depressing day if you insist on taking physical risks.

28th – A quiet day, when you will be able to please yourself. Loved ones will understand if you would rather not be involved in their plans. This evening should be spent in the company of friends.

29th – Good entertainment ideas made by those younger than yourself should be taken up. You may find the cost high, but you will gain an enormous amount of pleasure.

30th – The month ends on a depressing note. Overwork will make you tired and irritable. Members of your family and/or loved ones will not understand your behaviour.

October

1st – Today Mercury moves into Scorpio. This suggests that you will be greatly concerned with big business, insurance affairs, or perhaps with bureaucrats and officials. Not to worry, things should go your way.

2nd – Neptune finally decides to resume forward action, so work and career affairs should become less complicated in the near future.

3rd – The Moon in Taurus suggests that you should spend this Sunday rather quietly, as you are running out of energy fast. You could ask a friend around for a quiet drink, but do not encourage them to stay over-long.

4th – Relatives are not the best companions if making shopping expeditions – better to go with friends. This afternoon is the most favourable time to deal with purely personal matters.

5th – Colds and chills are likely to be contracted while on the move this Saturday, so care should be taken in this direction. The afternoon is good for physical pursuits.

6th – Neighbours and work colleagues should be invited to your home. You will glean some useful information with regard to your work-place.

7th – If you have not yet made plans for this week, then you should get down to it now. This is not a time to go off half-cocked. Plan a strict schedule and stick to it if you want to make progress.

8th – There are people around you who are trying to undermine your confidence. Therefore keep all that you are doing to yourself. Domestic partnerships are likely to explode this evening.

9th – Problems within the home are likely to have some bearing on the day's events. A friend's advice will be impractical and heavy-handed; you will have to follow your own counsel.

10th – Make the most of any help which is offered to you. This is a time for laying down a blueprint for the rest of your life. The only thing is that you must ensure that you stick to it.

11th – A good day for all those involved in the search for a financial loan. Banks and loan companies will have a ready smile and cash to offer. This evening is a favourable time to put domestic matters on a secure footing.

12th – Your travel plans will have to be rearranged to suit the needs of other people. Although this may annoy you, it would be better to go along with them unless you want to disappoint everyone.

13th – A quiet day when you will have plenty of time to yourself. If you are married, now is the time to discuss any differences of opinion you may have. Solutions can be found.

14th – A good day for putting short-term financial plans into operation. Small risks are all right, but do not invest the whole of your family fortune. Joint ventures are likely to pay off best.

15th – This is the day of the New Moon, and it falls in the fun area of your life. Therefore sports, children, socializing and romance are all highlighted and new beginnings can be expected.

16th – Venus moves into Libra, which will be good news for the Geminian involved in creativity. Over the next few weeks there should be several financial offers for you to consider.

17th – You will get through domestic jobs very quickly today, and will have plenty of time for enjoyment. Little things may go wrong, but provided you do not make a big song and dance about them, the day will be an enjoyable one.

18th – Some good opportunities are around for the enterprising Geminian. If you are willing to work hard and long, financial progress will be swift. Good news this evening comes from a relative.

19th – It is likely that affairs of the heart will take up much of your time – not only your own, but problems with younger members of the family.

20th – A good day for putting the minds of elderly relatives at ease. They may have suffered a health setback, and you will be needed to console and reassure them.

21st – You may have the feeling that you are doing all the donkey work; put this viewpoint to your colleagues in an effort to clear the air. You will get the cooperation you are looking for.

22nd – Do not allow relatives to take up any more of your time. They have been taking you for granted for far too long, and today is the time to put your foot down very firmly.

23rd – The Sun moves into Scorpio today, making it an ideal time for those professionally involved with mortgage companies, banks, the Stock Exchange or insurance. Likewise a good time for Geminians who are dealing with such people.

24th – The Moon in Aquarius suggests that the further you get away from your home base this Sunday, the happier you will be. You are in an adventurous mood, and may meet some interesting new people.

25th – A day for clearing out the dead wood. Outdated opinions and ideas will have to go in order to make way for the progressive and the new. Partners will be surprised at your ruthlessness.

26th – A day for the adventurous spirits. Make the most of invitations from friends who are usually more venturesome. Go along with their harebrained schemes for entertainment.

27th – Another day when you should be reckless, but only in spirit. Those working in and around the home will find that putting finishing touches to do-it-yourself jobs brings satisfaction.

28th – Ideas that you shelved some time ago should now be brought out, dusted down and put on display. You should be able to get the cooperation of those whose support you need.

29th – You may think it necessary to spend money in order to impress a superior. While this appears to be a wise move, however, you have no need to take such a course of action: it is not expected.

30th – This is the day of the Full Moon and it occurs in the part of your life devoted to the subconscious and self-undoing. Take care where important decisions are necessary over the next few days. Mistakes are a distinct possibility.

31st – You will have plenty of time to finish off all your outstanding jobs. Do not allow other people to make your work-load heavier. This evening is an excellent time to mix business with pleasure.

November

1st – Harebrained schemes put to you by colleagues will have no chance of succeeding, therefore keep your cash in your pocket. Housewives should not buy anything from doorstep salespeople.

2nd – Marriage difficulties could appear today. Arguments and disagreements arising now will take quite a time to sort out. Try to remain calm under all circumstances.

3rd – The atmosphere within your home base will be explosive. You should try not to antagonize anybody. Give the benefit of the doubt to those who are most argumentative.

4th – A very crowded day, when you will have to plan carefully if you are to get through all you hope to achieve. You may have to do some reorganizing in order to complete your jobs.

5th – Another day when it appears that there is too much to do. Try to delegate as much as possible. Those around will be cooperative, so you should not have too much trouble in offloading some tasks.

6th – Impulse could lead you into difficulties, especially where your actions are concerned. Try to keep a tight control. This afternoon is a good time for contacting people who have been elusive.

7th – Do not allow other people to impede your progress today.

You need as much freedom as possible in order to get through your social or romantic calendar. A short trip is likely at some point.

8th – The Moon in Virgo suggests a certain amount of activity on the home front. A good day for entertaining, then, or for making changes perhaps in preparation for next month's festive period.

9th – Mars moves into your opposition, and you begin a rather accident-prone period. Furthermore, relationships could become rather tense, so it is up to you to keep calm.

10th – Venus moves into Scorpio, which throws a rosy glow over the atmosphere at work and also your personal relationships. The chance of romance with a colleague blossoms.

11th – The big astrological news is that Jupiter has moved into Scorpio, so for the remainder of the year and early 1994 your good luck is to be found at work and within your relationships with colleagues. Lucky professions are those connected with the service industries and health.

12th – The Moon in Scorpio suggests that you will receive unexpected invitations to parties and to a social gathering. Be your usual adaptable self and accept.

13th – This is New Moon day, therefore a great time for tackling anything fresh – and that includes relationships. Someone new may enter your life; should this occur, they will be of a rather intense nature.

14th – The Moon is in your opposition, so there is no point in thinking you can get your own way in all directions. If you are in a relationship, for heaven's sake consult your opposite number.

15th – Someone in the working environment is enjoying the limelight, but stifle any envious feelings you may have and try to be happy for them instead.

16th – Mercury resumes forward action tomorrow, therefore you are advised to shelve anything important for the time being. Once this occurs, you will find progress that much easier to make.

17th – A little give and take is necessary today when dealing with those older than yourself. Relatives and workmates, especially older ones, will be cantankerous and very difficult to please.

18th – You will be feeling very restless during the early part of the day, and will achieve nothing as a result. Later, things brighten and you will zip through work you had left uncompleted.

19th – Those around you will, for once, be ready to cooperate with you. If you need favours, now is the time to ask for them. Financial losses are likely for those involved in the arts and literary professions.

20th – Friends or partners who have been obstructive will now come to your aid, so do not be afraid to ask for assistance whenever you need it. Things on the home front are still a trifle touchy where relatives are concerned.

21st – Keep your opinions and criticisms to yourself as they will not be well received. If visiting relatives or friends, do not push yourself to the fore; a back-seat ride is what you should aim for just now.

22nd – The Sun moves into your opposition today, and for the next month it is those who are able to cooperate the most who will benefit. An excellent time for the formation of professional partnerships.

23rd – Personal and domestic worries will come to a head today, but it looks as if this is for the general good. Partners will be willing to discuss all areas of conflict. Romance is not well-starred for the single.

24th – You will find that extra expenses are involved for children, so keep family entertainment to a minimum. Others will find that money leaves the pocket rather more quickly than the eye can see.

25th – Geminians in creative work should be able to put their talents to good use today. Those in physical jobs will be working much harder than of late, but financial rewards will come your way.

26th – Do not hesitate to put new ideas to work: you will probably find quicker ways of doing familiar jobs. Housewives are warned against inviting tradespeople into the home.

27th – Headaches could dog you today, therefore do not attempt any work that requires too much concentration or might cause eye-strain. Those working from home will be subject to constant interruptions.

28th – Ideally, this should be a quiet, lazy Sunday. Uncharacteristically, you are not full of the joys of living and rather feel like keeping your head down. Explain how you feel to your friends and partner.

29th – This is the day of the Full Moon and it occurs in your sign, indicating that a minor cycle in life is about to come to an end; there is little you can do about this except remain resilient.

30th – Domestic life is still prone to upheaval and argument, especially among the marrieds. Words spoken in haste will be regretted. Try to sort out your problems logically.

December

1st – Minor accidents could spoil your day and make things difficult for people around. Those out travelling on the roads are especially at risk, so observe all traffic regulations scrupulously.

2nd – Do not enter into joint financial gambling; also, keep expenditure to a minimum. This afternoon is the best time for making long-distance telephone calls.

3rd – Venus moves into your opposition and in doing so throws a golden glow over all existing relationships, both professional and personal. If you are single, you could very well meet someone important during the next few weeks.

4th – This is a particularly lucky day for those who have decided to get married: winter weddings and engagements are well-starred. The single will find a good deal of fun in visiting friends or relatives.

5th – Give older relatives the benefit of the doubt today, or you could find yourself in a difficult situation. Conflict is more than just a possibility.

6th – There is plenty of activity at home today, and also during the evening. Therefore, it is likely that you will be entertaining; if not, you can expect unexpected visitors.

7th – Mercury moves into your opposition, and stirs up your jangling nerves. You are going to need more rest than usual, so keep a healthy respect for your physical well-being and watch your diet.

8th – Not a day for falling in love, but rather a time for consolidating that which you already have. The single will need to give and take if they wish a relationship to blossom.

9th – A good day for housewives who are out hunting for bargains. The further you get away from your home base, the better. Commercial travellers and representatives will find new contacts.

10th – Someone will be out to pull the wool over your eyes and outsmart you where a business decision is concerned. Put the brakes on career matters at present.

11th – This may be a Saturday, but nevertheless it is likely that you will be bumping into or getting together with work contacts or colleagues. Better double-check that this does not clash with the plans your partner has already made.

12th – The Moon opposes you and stirs up your restlessness. There is no point in expecting a quiet Sunday – you will be fidgety and rather tetchy. The way to offset this is to go out for a nice long walk in the fresh air.

13th – This is the day of the New Moon and it falls in your opposition. If you are single, someone new and exciting could enter your life. For those in a steady relationship, a fresh set of circumstances rears its head.

14th – The festive season's shopping can be completed today by those with an eye for a bargain. Housewives are advised to check their change, as losses are indicated in this direction.

15th – Make all of your courtesy calls today as far as possible; you are in good spirits, and this applies equally to those you visit. This evening appears to be a time for family get-togethers.

16th – A great time for mixing business with pleasure – attending the office party or perhaps a festive lunch. If you are driving, however, you should watch your drink intake.

17th – Do not allow yourself to become complacent – you need to work for what you most desire. Help will come from unexpected quarters, and from the opposite sex.

18th – Finances take a beating today and partners will want to know why. Try to curb expenditure as much as possible. This evening is a very good time for making personal plans.

19th – Minor health problems will loom in the form of headaches and eyestrain. This is not the best day to attempt jobs that require concentration or attention to detail. Avoid do-it-yourself tasks, too.

20th – Mars moves into Capricorn, advising you to be watchful and take care that you do not fall foul of officials or bureaucrats. There is a slight chance that you could be too pushy and aggressive when in their company.

21st – Not a favourable day for last-minute Christmas shopping. Housewives will be frustrated in their attempts to find bargains. However, this evening is a good time for partying, so accept all invitations.

22nd – Those out on the road are advised to take extra care and observe traffic regulations; a minor brush with the law is likely. Others will find the day routine and quiet.

23rd – A good day for tracking down a superior who has been elusive for some time, also for asking favours from those you admire. This evening is a favourable time for romance.

24th – Parents will find children excitable and difficult to manage. Try to remember the time of the year, and you will understand their frame of mind. This is a very good evening for getting together with close friends and/or neighbours if you have time.

25th – MERRY CHRISTMAS! There appears to be little to mar your day, although there is a likelihood of over-indulgence. Care should be taken if travelling long distances. You may be a little depressed at some point, but soon allow loved ones to sweep this to one side.

26th – A stay-at-home day, when you will find much more amusement and entertainment within your own environment. Outside entertainment will come expensive and will not be up to standard.

27th – Mercury and Venus move into Capricorn, suggesting that at some time during the ensuing weeks those who work in big business, mortgage broking, the stock market or insurance can expect some good news.

28th – This is the day of the Full Moon, and it occurs in Cancer – the financial area of your life. Be watchful with possessions, and do not spend on unnecessary items which you can ill-afford.

29th – Do not try to cram too much into today, or you could end up irritable and touchy with those around. However, you may find it necessary to pay a visit to an elderly relative, which could take up much of your time.

30th – You will have finance on your mind, and could be feeling depressed at your own extravagance. Those looking for romance should find it this evening, but do not expect too much from any new relationship born today.

31st – A good day for putting yourself in the limelight. You will be on top form, and others will take to you. If attending parties this evening, make certain you are in full control of your faculties – minor accidents are likely. HAPPY NEW YEAR!

The Moon and Your Moods

Our moods are clearly affected by the Moon. After all, why on earth should such a well-balanced person as yourself be, on certain days, bad tempered, nervy, emotional, frigid and senti- mental? Well, I'm afraid it is all down to the man in the Moon. Prove it for yourself. Take a look at the Moon table then put it away for a month. In the meantime makes notes of your moods, then rescue the table and you will notice a clear pattern of behaviour. You don't need an astrologer to work out for you that, during the month whilst you were making notes, the Moon was in Scorpio when you were feeling depressed, in Cancer when you were feeling romantic, in Aries when you were bad tempered, et cetera. Your own individual pattern will be repeated each month; but do not be surprised if you are unaffec- ted when the Moon passes through, for example, Aries or Libra. Such a happening would merely indicate that these two signs are not particularly prominent on your birth chart.

Female readers would probably like to take a note of the fact that their menstrual cycle, if normal length, will begin when the Moon is in the same sign each month. Why not have a try? You could find out a lot about yourself.

Moon Tables and Your Moods 1993

Jan	Feb	Mar	Apr	May	June	July	Aug	Sept	Oct	Nov	Dec	
												1
												2
												3
												4
												5
												6
												7
												8
												9
												10
												11
												12
												13
												14
												15
												16
												17
												18
												19
												20
												21
												22
												23
												24
												25
												26
												27
												28
												29
												30
												31

Aries
Taurus
Gemini
Cancer
Leo
Virgo
Libra
Scorpio
Sagittarius
Capricorn
Aquarius
Pisces

Full and New Moons 1993

January	8th full in	Cancer
	22nd new in	Aquarius
February	6th full in	Leo
	21st new in	Pisces
March	8th full in	Virgo
	23rd new in	Aries
April	6th full in	Libra
	21st new in	Aries
May	6th full in	Scorpio
	21st new in	Gemini
June	4th full in	Sagittarius
	20th new in	Cancer
July	3rd full in	Capricorn
	19th new in	Cancer
August	2nd full in	Aquarius
	17th new in	Leo
September	1st full in	Pisces
	16th new in	Virgo
	30th full in	Aries
October	15th new in	Libra
	30th full in	Taurus
November	13th new in	Scorpio
	29th full in	Gemini
December	13th new in	Sagittarius
	28th full in	Cancer

Key

Aries	Leo	Sagittarius
Taurus	Virgo	Capricorn
Gemini	Libra	Aquarius
Cancer	Scorpio	Pisces

ADVERTISEMENT

YOUR BIRTH CHART
by TERI KING
A BOOK OF LIFE

Simply fill in your details on the form below for an interpretation of your birth chart compiled by TERI KING'S ASTROGEL. Your birth chart will be supplied bound and gold lettered 'My Book of Life'. Send this form, together with your cheque or postal order for £15.00 (fifteen pounds sterling) (inc. p&p) U.K. only. Overseas add £1.50 (one pound fifty pence sterling) for postage, payable to *ASTROGEL,* to: ASTROGEL, 6 ELM GROVE ROAD, BARNES, LONDON SW13 0BT, ENGLAND.

Date of birth ....Time of birth ....

Place of birth ....Country of birth ....

Name ....

Address ....

....

Postcode ....

A birth chart also makes an ideal present! Why not include, on a separate sheet, the details of a friend or member of your family? Include £15.00 for each extra chart.

Juliet Sharman-Burke

The Complete Book of Tarot £4.99

Tarot cards are like mirrors which reflect unsuspected knowledge deep in the unconscious mind. This teach yourself guide to reading the cards is designed to help activate and stimulate your innate sensitivity as a first step in developing intuition – the hallmark of the serious Tarot reader. Whether you want to interpret the cards for others, or use them to help gain a much deeper and more revealing understanding of yourself, you will find *The Complete Book of Tarot* both instructive and inspiring

Linda Goodman

Linda Goodman's Sun Signs £7.99

Have you ever wondered about yourself? What you are really like,
whether you'll make a good wife, mother or lover, whether other
people like you? Linda Goodman reveals the real you, your personality
and character as the stars see you, in this remarkably lively and
down-to-earth book.

Lori Reid

The Complete Book of the Hand £6.99

Let hand analysis help you take control of your life

Each individual palm is a unique register of past experiences and an indicator of future events. Your hand is one of the most valuable tools for self-assessment, providing vital clues to understanding your psyche.

Lori Reid adopts a scientific approach to hand analysis. She traces its ancient roots, then describes its modern techniques and contemporary uses.

The Complete Book of the Hand looks at every aspect of the hand – from its potential in medical diagnoses to what it can reveal about character and personality, about relationships, career prospects, health and significant events in your life.

Jacqueline Stallone

Star Power £5.99

Find Out
* How the stars helped Jacqueline's son Sylvester hit the big time . . .

* Your rating on the Stallone love scale

* Why Leos Madonna and Sean Penn should never have gone on a second date . . .

* Your best bet careers

Packed with celebrity gossip STARPOWER explores not just the traditional 12 divisions of the zodiac, but the 36 sub-categories that make all the difference in discovering hidden personality strengths . . . and dangers.

Jacqueline Stallone knows that STARPOWER has worked for her – and for her famous son. She's convinced it has worked for Hollywood's brightest stars. Now she shows you how it can work for YOU!

All Pan books are available at your local bookshop or newsagent, or can be
ordered direct from the publisher. Indicate the number of copies required and
fill in the form below.

Send to: **CS Department, Pan Books Ltd., P.O. Box 40,
             Basingstoke, Hants.   RG21 2YT.**

or phone: 0256 469551 (Ansaphone), quoting title, author
             and Credit Card number.

Please enclose a remittance* to the value of the cover price plus: 60p for the
first book plus 30p per copy for each additional book ordered to a maximum
charge of £2.40 to cover postage and packing.

*Payment may be made in sterling by UK personal cheque, postal order,
sterling draft or international money order, made payable to Pan Books Ltd.

Alternatively by Barclaycard/Access:

Card No. | | | | | | | | | | | | | | | | |

Signature:

Applicable only in the UK and Republic of Ireland.

*While every effort is made to keep prices low, it is sometimes necessary to
increase prices at short notice. Pan Books reserve the right to show on
covers and charge new retail prices which may differ from those advertised
in the text or elsewhere.*

NAME AND ADDRESS IN BLOCK LETTERS PLEASE:

....

Name ————————————————————————————

Address ——————————————————————————

————————————————————————————————

————————————————————————————————

————————————————————————————————

3/87